THE EMPIRICAL STUDY OF THE PSYCHOLOGY OF
RELIGION AND SPIRITUALITY IN
JAPAN

© 2020 Masami Takahashi. All rights reserved. No part of this book may be scanned, copied, uploaded or reproduced in any form or by any means, photographically, electronically or mechanically, without written permission from the copyright holder.

ISBN: 978-1-943492-80-0

Cover design by DesignPanache

Elm Grove Publishing | San Antonio, Texas | www.elmgrovepublishing.com
Elm Grove Publishing is a legally registered trade name of Panache Communication Arts, Inc.

THE EMPIRICAL STUDY OF THE PSYCHOLOGY OF
RELIGION AND SPIRITUALITY IN
JAPAN

Edited by
Masami Takahashi, Ph.D.

Foreword by
Ralph W. Hood, Jr.

The Empirical Study of the Psychology of Religion and Spirituality in Japan

While almost everyone in Japan regularly participates in traditional activities that are religious and spiritual in nature, it is perplexing that only 20 to 30% of the population self-identify with a particular religion. Several accounts have been offered to explain this discrepancy, but these speculations had never been examined empirically. There are several reasons as to why Japanese empirical scientists ignored the topic for so long. One may be that Japanese scientists themselves are too accustomed to the tradition to reflect upon the discrepancy. Since even astute researchers may fail to recognize such a fertile field for empirical research, the opportunities and venues to pursue this line of research in Japanese academia have been scarce.

The Empirical Study of the Psychology of Religion and Spirituality in Japan is a translated version of the original book, a collection of chapters by scholars from different psychological disciplines. It is the first book with an emphasis on empirical perspectives on the topic. Thus, it is also the first book written in English in the field. This book offers not only detailed empirical data, but also an examination of the theories and ideologies that underlie contemporary understanding of religion and spirituality in Japan.

Contents

List of Contributors — 9

Translators — 10

Foreword
    Ralph W. Hood, Jr. — 11

Editor's Note, English Language Edition
    Masami Takahashi — 15

Preface
    Kobo Matsushima, Daisuke Kawashima and *Ryo Nishiwaki*
    Editors, Japanese Language Edition — 17

Introduction
    Measuring Japanese People's Religiosity: Guidelines for Studying the Psychology of Religion and Spirituality *Kobo Matsushima* — 21

1. **Exploring Japanese Religiosity after the Great East Japan Earthquake of 2011: Memorializing Tragic Deaths of Children** *Tetsuo Ohmura* — 37

2. **Role of Religion in the Aftermath of a Major Disaster: A Lesson from the Great Hanshin-Awaji Earthquake**
Daisuke Kawashima and *Yu Urata* — 57

3. **People Living in Faith Traditions: Understanding the Meaning of "Faith" in Japan** *Shuki Aizawa* — 71

4. **Japanese Religiosity through the Lens of Psychological Health: The Role of Religion in Seeking a Better Life** *Masahiro Nakao* — 86

5. **Finding Religion in Nature: An Alternative Index of Religiosity** *Ryo Nishiwaki*   102

6. **Hidden *Shinto* Narrative in Japanese Culture: A Religion that is Too Ubiquitous** *Katsuya Sakai*   118

7. **Unfolding Religiosity in Japan: An Exploration of the Images of Spirituality** *Masaki Kobayashi*   136

8. **The World of Religion Among Those Who Claim to Be Non-Religious** *Ayumu Arakawa*   144

9. **Spirituality: Exploring Its Complexity and Potentials in Psychology** *Masami Takahashi*   155

Appendix
Kobo Matsushima   171

References
    175

List of Contributors

Shuki Aizawa
Atomi University

Ayumu Arakawa
Musashino Art University

Daisuke Kawashima
Chukyo University

Masaki Kobayashi
Chuo Academic Research Institute

Kobo Matsushima
The University of Tokyo

Masahiro Nakao
Osaka Ohtani University

Ryo Nishiwaki
Nanzan University

Tetsuo Ohmura
Tohoku University

Katsuya Sakai
Izumo Shrine Yawaragi Branch

Masami Takahashi
Northeastern Illinois University

Yu Urata
Osaka University

Translators

Hanna O. Krieg
Kobe Shoin Women's University

Masami Takahashi
Northeastern Illinois University

Ilja Musulin
Center for Global Studies on Culture and Society,
College of Economics, Nihon University

Ayaka Kasuga
Graduate School of Human Sciences,
Osaka University

Foreword

by *Ralph W. Hood, Jr.*

It is my honor to write this introduction to this careful English translation of *Shukyo wo shinrigaku suru* published in 2016. Translated literally the title has issues that might suggest a less than empirical approach to religion. This book is committed to empirical studies of religion in Japan, but as with the study of religion in America, psychologists have found it necessary to add "spirituality" a term that is difficult to translate into Japanese, especially as there is no noun for this term in Japanese. However, the editors note that the literal translation "Psychologizing of religion" would be far less appropriate. Thus, the very American title of *The Empirical Study of the Psychology of Religion and Spirituality in Japan* is more than appropriate for this study. This book is the result of a three-year study to measure Japanese religiosity empirically by methods championed in the West. Yet while American empirical psychology dominates the psychology of religion and spirituality in the West, the editors and authors of this book have not blindly followed American positivistic empirical methods when they are less than appropriate.

The necessary empirical measures and purely quantitative data are carefully documented in the Appendix. However, each chapter explores by mixed methods this three-year project (Japan Multidimensional Assessment of Religion and Spirituality or J-MARS) begun in the spring of 2012 that has done much more than simply measure Japanese religiosity.

Collectively these chapters introduce English readers to what Japan shares with America, but the empiricism is more in the tradition of

William James and of his justly famous *Varieties of Religious Experience* (1902) than the positivistic naturalism of the *Principles of Psychology* (1890) found to be too limiting, even more strikingly so when abridged as *Psychology: The Briefer Course* (1892). These researchers have not simply been bound by a narrowly conceived empirical positivism that has begun to characterize much of American empirical psychology. To cite but one example, in a popular text of William James' writings (1902-1910) is a brief essay where he explores his own reaction to the great San Francisco earthquake and fire in 1906. In it he notes how inadequate objective scientific descriptions are in a purely positivistic sense, in the face of what appears to "untutored men" as supernatural warnings or retributions (James, 1907/1987, p.1217).

Earthquakes plague Japan like California. Two studies in this text employ empirical methods including quantitative, ethnographic, semi-structured interviews to study the survivors of Japan's Great Hanshin-Awaji earthquake of 1995. Here we understand the Japanese sense of "psychologizing religion" as genuine human, non-rational responses to earthquakes. James documents his own reactions consistent with Japanese concerns: "Do not forget." This is the appropriate empirical descriptor, a psychological response not captured in merely positivistic language. Likewise, in a study of the Great Japanese earthquake of 2011 there is careful documentation giving rise to non-rational means of memorializing the dead, in which elementary school graduations were cancelled and diplomas were awarded to the dead. Here the troublesome phrase in English, "psychologizing religion," gains some usefulness as we learn how the tradition of awarding diplomas to the dead occurs in other cultures, including America. This non-rational "psychologizing" is precisely in line with the kind of genuine empirical psychology William James argued would make the psychological study of "spirituality" if not religion truly empirical.

Throughout this thoughtful text the empirical emphasis is maintained, but we are also continually reminded that some terms simply do not travel well cross-culturally. Faith is one such term, that is more problematic in Japan than in America. Empirical comparisons across diverse religious groups common to Japan (such as Buddhism, Christianity, and *Shintoism*) reveal a more complex mosaic of traditions unlike America which, as its psychology of religion remains heavily influenced by Protestantism and a self-conscious religious identity more common than in

Japan, which even in international surveys is an outlier. However, this is not to say that Japanese do not have a wide variety of rituals and practices, that again justify the identification of a wide variety of practices and beliefs if not strictly religious are properly identified as spiritual when operationalized and empirically documented. Of interest, given greater diversity of faith traditions in Japan and of less personal faith identification, are the documentation of various empirical differences between these groups.

A consistent theme throughout all these carefully crafted chapters is attention to mixed methods when quantitative empirical data are interpreted in light of the participants' own understandings. Here again, the empirical methods are not naively imposed, but consistent with William James is the extensive use of in-depth quotes on how the Japanese best characterize their faith. There is a parallel by Masaharu Anesaki in his widely read study of *Nichren: The Buddhist Prophet* (1916, p. v) that shows, even when American concepts seem poorly suited for Japan, the radical empiricism championed by William James is an empirical method that does justice to understanding the complexities of great personalities struggling with, if not religion, then spirituality. So when we learn that Hitler and Hussein are seen as more spiritual for Japanese than Americans, we know that given there is no equivalent term in Japanese for the English noun "spirituality," we must not rely simply on statistically significant differences, but also interviews, so that words can be placed within context of the specific culture studied. Thus, in other chapters, data on the meaning of faith in Japanese issues of religion and psychological health, and powerful experiences in nature are explored using mixed methods that clearly establish that the psychology of religion and spirituality in Japan has its own unique contribution to make to the accumulating body of empirical work. Overall, each of the authors has done a great service in bringing this English translation to press. If the grant from the Japan Society for the Promotion of Science (JSPS) was to "measure religiosity," this book achieves that and so much more. The empirical study of religion and spirituality in Japan has a bright future.

Sources:

Anesaki, M. (1916). *Nichiren: The Buddhist Prophet*. Cambridge, MA: Harvard University Press.
James, W. (1892). *Psychology: The briefer course*. New York: Henry Holt.
James, W. (1890/1981). *The Principles of psychology*. Cambridge, MA: Harvard University Press.
James, W. (1902/1985). *The varieties of religious experience. A study in human nature.* Cambridge, MA: Harvard University Press.
James, W. (1907/1987). *On some mental effects of the earthquake. William James – writings 1902-1910*, (pp. 1215-1222). New York: The Library of America University Press.

Editor's Note, English Language Edition

The Japanese Society for Study of Psychology of Religion (JSSPR) (https://psychology-of-religion-japan.org/index.html), a consortium of social scientists and religious scholars, was founded in 2003 to advance research in the complex nature of religion and spirituality in contemporary Japan. In the following years, its core members played an important role in revitalizing the field by organizing seminars and symposia at various professional conferences, and eventually published *Shinrigaku-gairon* [*The Study of Psychology and Religion*, 2011], the first comprehensive book on the topic in Japan since 1946.

As a part of the JSSPR's effort, the Japan Multidimensional Assessment of Religion and Spirituality (J-MARS) was implemented in 2012. This project included an investigation into attitudes toward religions among various cohorts from school-aged children to older adults, into ad hoc religious rituals carried out by the survivors of major natural disasters such as the Hanshin-Awaji earthquake in 1995 and the Great East Japan earthquake in 2011, and into the unique conceptualizations of contemporary Japanese spirituality. The effort culminated in the publication of another book, *Shukyo wo shinrigaku suru*, in 2016.

This volume is an English translation of the 2016 book, which is primarily based on the J-MARS data. Here, I tried to preserve the essence of the original book as much as possible, but that required modifying a few things. First, although the literal translation of the original book title was *Psychologizing Religion*, I changed it to *The Empirical Study of the Psychology of Religion and Spiritualty in Japan*. In Japanese, "psychologizing" is a catchy and novel phrase without any Freudian connotations, and the original editors thought it was suitable for a book that was marketed to the general public. Also, despite the extensive discussion of spirituality, the original title did not include spirituality because of the non-scientific, cultish nuances associated with the term in the contemporary Japan. Thus, the new title is less catchy but reflects the book contents more accurately.

Second, due to the differences between English and Japanese linguistic rules, their differing conventions in the logical structure of writing, and variation in what assumed to be common knowledge in Japanese and English-speaking societies, I had to modify some parts of the original to "fit" the conventions familiar to the English-speaking readers. This includes moving some sections around to make the discussions flow more smoothly and replacing some of the Japanese expressions with ones that are more common in the West.

Third, the translation for *kami* requires some explanation. In this volume, when the context is specific to the Judeo-Christianity or Islam, I used "the God" to denote a specific deity. On the other hand, the term "gods" is used when the original reference is in the plural (i.e., "*kami-gami*") or the context is related to *Shintoism* and Buddhism or is unspecified. The common Japanese expression of *shin-butsu* denoting *Shinto* gods and the Buddha was simply translated as "god/Buddha."

Fourth, I added several new photographs that I thought might help the non-Japanese readers gain a better understanding of the on-going discussion. *Seishin-Shobo*, the original publisher, was gracious enough to allow me to make this modification.

*****

I would like to express my deep gratitude to Ms. Yuki Ishimaru, Dr. Janet Fair-Christianson, and Dr. Phyllis Lyons for their input in the translation process. Special thanks are also due to Ms. Brittany Burns for editing. I also like to thank Northeastern Illinois University and the University of Tokyo for their generous support. Finally, I am greatly indebted to Mick and Diane Prodger of Elm Grove Publishing for their editorial and publication expertise.

Masami Takahashi
February 2020

Preface

    This book focuses on a topic that may not be familiar to readers, "the empirical study of the psychology of religion and spirituality." Most readers are probably not familiar with the term and may be thinking to themselves that they have never seen a book with such a theme. The empirical psychology of religion and spirituality is a branch of psychology that studies empirically matters pertaining to religion. It is the practice of discussing religion based on empirical data obtained through research, or to put it more simply, studying religion by relying on data as the source of information.

    The field of the empirical psychology of religion and spirituality in Japan has long been stagnant. Numerous handbooks on other topics in psychology are prominently displayed on the shelves of Japanese bookstores, but in fact, only two handbooks exist on the empirical psychology of religion: Megumi Imada's *Psychology of Religion* (Bunsendo Publishing, 1946) and Satoru Kaneko's *Introduction to the Psychology of Religion* (Nakanishiya Publishing, 2011). This book addresses a serious gap in Japanese scholarship.

    Why has the empirical psychology of religion and spirituality been so little explored in Japan? Many factors can be considered, but the main one is that studying Japanese religiosity and spirituality psychologically is difficult. The religious landscape in Japan is complex, and the way faith is expressed is also varied, making it difficult—even for Japanese researchers—to pinpoint some generalized sense of religion of the Japanese. This becomes a large obstacle for psychological research, which moves in the direction of generalizability and universalization. What tends to happen is that, when one tries to pursue the religiosity and spirituality of the Japanese, one runs into the wall of the multiplicity of Japan's religious landscape, thus making it difficult to conduct the research. In addition, even with the existing studies, discussion and exchange (coordination and collaboration) between researchers has been rare, and research results tend to stand in isolation. As a result, empirical studies of the psychology of religion and spirituality in Japan as a field has continued to languish.

However, over time new attempts to psychologically understand Japanese religiosity and spirituality have begun. One such example is the launch of the Society for the Study of Psychology of Religion in 2003. As its various activities have accumulated, mutual coordination and cooperation in such research has heightened. Furthermore, due to the unprecedented earthquake of March 11, 2011, more than ever before, the Japanese have found themselves forced to face questions of their own spirituality, such as the meaning of life or death. As a result, interest in the religiosity and spirituality, as well as in mental health, has grown significantly, leading to a groundswell in the psychological investigation of those issues as well.

Wishing to establish a comprehensive project that would psychologically examine Japanese religiosity and spirituality and further the understanding of their relation to mental health, while effectively using the human network of the Society for the Study of Psychology of Religion, we undertook the "Japan Multidimensional Assessment of Religion and Spirituality" (J-MARS) project. The J-MARS project received a grant from the Japan Society for the Promotion of Science (JSPS) and, starting in April 2012, conducted research activities for three years. The official project title was, "The Relation between Religiosity/Spirituality and Mental Health: An Empirical Study of Hardships and Resilience," Grants-in-Aid for Scientific Research, category B, for the fiscal year 2012; Principal Investigator Kobo Matsushima, (Reg. No. 24330185). The J-MARS project was built on our experience of past accomplishments and gaps in the study of Japanese empirical psychology of religion research. This book recounts the difficulties the field has always faced in capturing the religiosity and spirituality of the Japanese people, and the foundational advances achieved during the three years of the J-MARS project.

In the field of psychology, it has long been said that the religiosity and spirituality of the Japanese people are difficult to grasp. In our opinion, such a complex study topic cannot be understood in detail if we keep trying to comprehend it based on some broad and imprecise framework of what the Japanese are like. If we approach research through generalizations and search for universals in the objects or phenomena under study, as is customary in psychology, the research object we are trying to comprehend may further elude us, and we may actually end up concluding that the religiosity and spirituality of the Japanese are too difficult to grasp.

In order to break out of this circular argument, we propose that the object of research be defined more clearly. That is, we believe that it is necessary to build research upon defining as clearly as possible the object we wish to investigate. Since all religious groups, denominations, or sects have their own idiosyncrasies, this means that when we study religions such as Christianity, Buddhism or *Shinto*, we must narrow the object of our study to the particularities of each group, denomination or sect. The same applies to studies whose research subjects are not believers of a particular religion. Thus, if for example we wish to study "the main forms of Japanese religious practice," such as paying respect to ancestral graves, the first visit of the year to a shrine or temple, the worship at *Shinto* and Buddhist home altars (prayers), or the so-called "spiritual boom" in Japanese popular culture, we must clarify the object of research as much as possible and build our research around it. This approach means designing the axis of research starting from the research object. For, if the object of research is clearly defined, then the domain associated with the object will also become clear and the phenomena we are trying to comprehend will inevitably emerge more saliently.

We believe that now is the time to accrue data using the approach we proposed in order to overcome the vagueness in existing descriptions of Japanese religiosity. This book takes a first step in that direction. The method taken by this volume is to clearly define the research objects, divide them into certain clusters, and look for the type of religiosity characteristic of each cluster. We believe that religiosity common to each cluster of questions will surface through such a procedure. We think that only when insights about such common features of religiosity are accumulated will some generalizable description of Japanese religiosity become visible. In other words, we wish to argue about Japanese religiosity inductively. This book does announce rather boldly our intention to "measure Japanese religiosity," but the reality is that we are engaged in collecting a multiplicity of research observations. We want the reader to be mindful that we do not intend to present generalized arguments about Japanese mentality and religiosity.

This book is about the empirical study of the psychology of religion and spirituality based not only on theories but also on factual data. In each chapter, we use the necessary psychological methods to approach the phenomenon or object in question and to conduct analysis and investigation. The judgment regarding what method to employ has been entrusted to each author. For that reason, some variation in the unity of the entire book may remain. But we want to demonstrate to readers that the psychology of religion means dealing with diversity and implies the existence of many different theories and methods of treating religion. Therefore, we ask readers to kindly understand that the approach and the presentation of the material will differ from chapter to chapter. We would be happy if this book provides readers with the opportunity to learn about different aspects of Japanese religiosity. And we also hope that readers will see that the empirical study of the psychology of religion and spirituality is an effective means of approaching Japanese religiosity and carries various possibilities within it.

Finally, we would like to cordially thank the publishing house Seishin Shobo, which originally published this study advancing the field of the empirical psychology of religion and spirituality, and Yuriko Matsuyama from the editorial department, from whom we received much advice and warm encouragement throughout this journey.

Kobo Matsushima, Daisuke Kawashima and Ryo Nishiwaki
Editors, Japanese Language Edition
July 2016

Introduction

Measuring Japanese People's Religiosity: Guidelines for Studying the Psychology of Religion and Spirituality

Kobo Matsushima, The University of Tokyo

1. For Studying the Psychology of Religion and Spirituality

Studying the psychology of religion and spirituality of the Japanese. Is that even possible? In this chapter, I will explain what kind of perspective and thinking are necessary to study the psychology of religion and spirituality, particularly from the following three viewpoints:

1) *Thinking based on the concept of religiosity*
2) *Grasping religiosity from the perspective of human development (temporally)*
3) *Addressing religiosity as a personal trait that any human being possesses*

From these perspectives, I will state the reason *why* it is possible to study the psychology of religion and spirituality.

First, I will describe the actual state of Japanese religiosity and provide the footing for studying the psychology of religion by examining it. Table 1 shows the results of opinion polls (international comparisons and domestic surveys) conducted by different institutions and newspaper companies.[1] To the question about whether or not they have a religion or faith, many Japanese answer "I do not," with the positive response rate concerning active involvement and membership in a religious group

Table 1 Japanese Religiosity

I. Religiosity of the Japanese as seen from international comparison surveys	
Religious consciousness	1. As for religious consciousness as a whole, the Japanese, in comparison with people from other countries, score high on reverence for ancestors and magical concepts, such as divination and fortune telling, spells or supernatural punishment.
	2. The Japanese tend to think that a "religious mindset" is important.
	3. The Japanese score low on other items regarding religious consciousness.
Religious behavior	1. Scores on magical acts involving amulets, talismans, fortune slips and fortune telling are relatively high in comparison with other countries.
	2. Scores on other types of religious behavior are on the whole low.
Religious consciousness and behavior among older adults	1. Scores concerning the mental aspect, such as those regarding the importance of "religious mindset" or the existence of a world after death, are not low in comparison with other nations.
	2. Scores on whether the respondents are religious, believe in a religion or conduct religious activities are low in comparison with other countries.
Home education	Home education related to religious development of children is not regarded as important.
II. Religiosity of the Japanese as seen from domestic surveys	
Religious or non-religious	1. The response rate varies depending on the text of the survey questions, but when it comes to active involvement and membership in religious organizations, it is low, at 10% (In some surveys the result hovers between 20% and 30%).
	2. Regarding the time of conversion, the percentage of those who came to have religious beliefs in childhood as a result of family influence and those who converted in adolescence is almost the same.
Interest in religion and the degree of importance attached to it	These fluctuate between 10% and 30%, which is, in general, low. The response to the items asking about the personal involvement is especially low.
Attitudes towards established religions	1. The negative image tends to be slightly higher than the positive.
	2. However, what functions as a factor contributing to such negative image are "financial profiteering" and "coercive persuasion to join," and not a perceived irrationality of that religion.
	3. The degree of trust in "religious groups" in general is low. Also, the trust in "new religions" is low.
Concepts such as deities, buddhas, and spirits	1. The percentage of those who affirm these beings is 30% to 40%, which is higher than the proportion of those who have joined a religious group or actively believe in a religion.
	2. When the content of the questions is not limited to "deities, buddhas and spirits," but is expanded to encompass the concepts of "supernatural power, destiny and karma," the positive response increases to between 60% and 70%.
Religious behavior	1. The proportion of those engaging in customary behavior, such as visiting graves, visiting temples and shrines at the beginning of the new year or participation in religious festivals as local events, is high (50% to 70%).
	2. Between 50% and 60% reply that they have had the experience of worshipping (praying) at a Shinto or Buddhist altar.
	3. The proportion of those engaging in behavior related to worldly benefits (amulets, talismans, prayers in Shinto shrines, etc.) is 20-30%.
	4. The percentage of those practicing religious action for which daily and spontaneous motivation is required (reading religious books, mental concentration, religious service or propagation) is low: from less than 10% to below 20%.

(Adopted from Nishiwaki, 2004)

standing at approximately 10%, although in some surveys it fluctuates between 20% and 30%. Such results show that a lot of Japanese people strongly believe that they are non-religious.

However, that the respondents declare themselves non-religious does not mean that the relationship between the Japanese and religion has been severed. Rather, the reality is the opposite. Take another look at Table 1, especially at the questions other than the one about whether or not one has a religion or faith. From them the involvement in and the inclination towards matters regarding religion can be seen. It seems that the Japanese are involved in and devoted to a rich variety of religion-related affairs. Why is it then, that they declare themselves to be "non-religious"? This is probably because the majority of them draw the conclusion that they are non-religious because they do not belong to a specific religion (religious group), or have no specific faith, and that, by extension, leads to the conclusion that the Japanese as a whole are non-religious. Of course, numerous books that argue about the grounds and the historical background of the thinking and discourse that the Japanese are non-religious have been published. However, there are probably not so many of those who still profess that they are non-religious or talk about how the Japanese are non-religious. That is, as Kan (2015) remarked, Japanese "non-religiosity" is more like a "state of thought suspension, which is far from describing them as atheist, since atheists unequivocally state that there is no God" (Figure 1).

Figure 1 *Rich variety of religions. Photo by Masami Takahashi*

Considering this situation, I would like to propose that we step back from thinking based on the criterion of having or not having faith in a particular religion. Doing so could make Japanese religiosity more visible than ever. Furthermore, a perspective different from the one focusing on the presence of faith in a particular religion could also make visible the rich religiosity among those who regard themselves as non-religious. Faith is an important element when thinking about religion, but not being constrained solely by that and acknowledging other elements on the same footing as faith would enable us to see the religiosity of Japanese people in a different light from before.

Those who wish to declare themselves as non-religious, may do so. Those who wish to make known that they have come to believe in a religion may do so. Either position is fine the way it is, but as a new way of looking at things, I would like to suggest considering not just faith, but also involvement and devotion in regard to other elements. Thus, I wish to propose that we try to grasp Japanese people's religiosity from a broader perspective, and not just as the question of whether someone believes in a particular religion or not. And, indeed, this is the perspective from which this book attempts to examine the inside workings and the outside appearance of the religiosity of Japanese people from various aspects. There are different ways to make such an attempt, but in this volume, we shall approach it by way of psychological science.

Approaching the subject via psychological science implies empirical inquiry, and empirical inquiry means arguing based on empirical data. That is what the psychological study of religion and spirituality aspires to do. In this chapter, based on the concept of religiosity, I wish to discuss what kind of perspective or thinking makes the study of the psychology of religion and spirituality possible.

2. Religiosity as a Psychological Construct
2.1 What is Religion?

How should studies be designed to examine the psychology of religion and spirituality? I will explain this by focusing on the concept of religiosity that forms its basis.

A) *The definition of religiosity*

Religiosity is a concept that denotes the degree of involvement in and devotion to religion in an individual. That is, religiosity is an index that measures how involved a person is in religion and denotes the extent to which an individual believes and feels (religious consciousness), and acts with regard to religion (religious practice).

Religious studies scholar Kishimoto (1961) defined religious consciousness as "something like covert behavior in religious practice including religious experience, primarily consisting of affective experience (emotion and will), and religious contemplation (intellect)." He further defined religious practice as "overt behavior in the practice strongly affected by social elements, such as rituals or propagation and missionary work." Thus, according to Kishimoto's definition, religious consciousness is a concept that includes a cognitive component (believing), which involves religious belief and knowledge, and an emotional component (feeling), which involves affective experience (religious experience), and a behavioral component (conduct) referring to religious practice. In other words, religiosity is a framework that encompasses religious consciousness and religious behavior.

B) *Explanation of religiosity by Glock*

While research on religiosity is wide-ranging, many scholars regard Glock's (1962) five religious dimensions as fundamental: knowledge, belief, experience, practice, and effects. "Knowledge" refers to possessing information on religious doctrines and doctrinal scriptures, "belief" to believing in religious teachings, "experience" includes conversion and denotes having religious experiences and emotions, while "practice" refers to specific religious behavior, such as worship or praying. Furthermore, "effects" refers to the social and secular influence that the above four dimensions have on the life, behavior, and mental state of believers. Effects are further divided into rewards and responsibilities. Rewards denote the peace of mind, deliverance from distress, a feeling of happiness, etc., while "responsibilities" refer to the acceptance of ethical prohibitions and fulfilling one's duties within the religious collective.

With the above in mind, I have illustrated the structure of religiosity in Table 2. Religiosity, thus, is a word that signifies "knowing (knowledge), believing (belief), feeling and experiencing (experience), and behaving (practice) in matters regarding religion,[2] as well as being influenced by the four dimensions (effects)."

Table 2 Structure of Religiosity

Religious consciousness	Cognitive component	Knowledge and belief	Effects (Reward and responsibility)
	Emotional component	Experience	
Religious behavior	Behavioral component	Practice	

C) *Religiosity regardless of one's belief in a particular religion*

In many cases, those who regard themselves as non-religious feel that they have no religion because they do not belong to any particular religious group. The criterion here is whether someone believes in the teachings of a particular religious group or not, so in the case where a closed-ended survey is conducted, the response is either "I believe" or "I do not believe." Furthermore, "I believe" is often interpreted as believing "continuously for a relatively extended period of time." I think that most Japanese respondents think of Christians as those who have relatively long-term commitment and that if the respondents do not have such a commitment, they end up claiming themselves to be non-religious.

As seen from the above, many Japanese seem to take having faith, believing, and believing continuously as indicators for being religious. However, I have doubts about whether believing should be the only indicator when it comes to being religious. That is, individuals' involvement and devotion in matters regarding religion (religiosity) is not limited solely to believing (belief), but also includes knowing (knowledge), feeling and experiencing (experience), behaving (practice), and undergoing the influence of these four dimensions (effects). In other words, believing (belief) is but one dimension of religiosity and other dimensions are its constituents as well. And while there are individual differences in the depth and degree concerning each of the dimensions, very many people are involved in and devoted to matters regarding religion. To be sure, believing is the central or core dimension of religiosity, but there are other considerations. That is why topics such as "People Living in Faith Traditions" (Chapter 3), and "People Who Claim to be Non-religious" (Chapter 8) are included in this book as well.

Many Japanese are too caught up in "believing" or to be more exact, in "believing continuously" when thinking about religiosity and specific religious groups. Would it not be good to pay more attention to knowing, feeling and experiencing, acting, and being influenced by these? When we see shrines, temples, and other religious edifices, we experience a feeling of sacredness, and when we find ourselves before the vastness of nature, we somehow experience a feeling of warmth and serenity. We also worship at *Shinto* and Buddhist altars and pay visits to graves as part of Buddhist memorial services. Furthermore, I have mentioned that there is excessive adherence to the importance of continuous belief, but when we go to shrines or temples to make a wish about passing an exam or receiving blessings for love or marriage, we earnestly pray that our prayers be answered, do we not? This thought that we want our prayers to be realized actually falls into the category of belief. And while it is by no means a continuous belief, I think that within these practices, doubtlessly, exists an earnest desire to believe.

Each of these examples truly reveals the inside workings and the outside appearance of religiosity. Furthermore, Table 1 clearly shows how broadly and deeply Japanese people are involved in matters regarding religion. Regardless of whether the persons involved realize it or not, those matters exist close to us. In this book we examine Japanese people's religiosity from the standpoint that such things exist close to us whether the persons involved realize it or not (We examine what has become apparent in disaster-stricken areas: the Great East Japan Earthquake of 2011 (Chapter 1) and the Great Awaji-Hanshin Earthquake (Chapter 2), as well as the religious view of nature (Chapter 5), the *Shinto* narrative (Chapter 6), and spirituality in Japan (Chapter 9)).

Consequently, the effort to achieve an understanding from the viewpoint of religiosity and not from whether or not a person believes in a particular religion should also bring to light the inside workings and the outside appearance of the religiosity of those who see themselves as non-religious. If we remove the shackles of insistence on continuous belief and approach the actual situation by examining the five dimensions of knowledge, belief, experience, practice and effects, the religiosity of the Japanese that has hitherto been invisible will be unveiled.

2.2 Approaching Religiosity from the Viewpoint of Human Development (the Temporal Axis)

"Human development" involves changes throughout life, from conception to death. Here "development" means diverse changes that happen to individuals in all of the following phases: before birth, infancy, toddlerhood, childhood, adolescence, adulthood, and old age (Takahashi, 2012). In other words, development implies "looking at humans temporally" (Koyasu, 2011). In this section I would like to consider religiosity from the viewpoint of human development (temporal axis), which constitute one prerequisite basis for the study of the psychology of religion.

Table 3 Three Concepts of Development

Model	Development in and after adulthood	Illustration of the developmental path	The role of age	Important dimension
Development as growth and socialization	Not possible		Extremely important	Body
Development as a lifelong process	Possible		Important	Social role
Development as self-actualization	Possible		Not so important	Mind

(Hori, 1991)

Hori (1991) defines human development as "a process of unfolding potentials over time" and proposes following three views (See Table 3):

1) Development as growth and socialization: This is a view of development that emphasizes biological and physiological conditions and regards development as a process lasting until one becomes an adult. Here, the aspect of life in which we become a biologically complete being is viewed as development. This perspective, however, makes considering development across a lifespan difficult because regular changes that take place after adulthood are simply regarded as decline or aging. Many developmental psychologists in the past have, more or less, held this perspective.
2) Development as a lifelong process: This is a view of development that stresses social processes and social roles (e.g., R. J. Havighurst's Developmental Tasks Theory). Theories of development that focus on changes in social roles aim to shed light on the course of the entire life and the sets of tasks that lie before us during the process, rather than focusing on the process of becoming an adult. Theories of family life cycle and career life cycle are a part of this perspective.
3) Development as self-actualization: This is a view that emphasizes the human mind and the dimension of the ego. Generally speaking, when one passes through adulthood, physiological functioning declines and one's social role declines, but while accepting those facts, it is possible to think that our ego can still grow beyond that point (e.g., C. G. Jung and E. H. Erikson).

Given the three concepts of development presented by Hori (1991), I think that religiosity could be categorized as "Development as self-actualization." [3] Regarding research on the development of religiosity, Nishiwaki (2005) states that "the quest for the answer to the question of what kind of developmental change human religiosity undergoes in mental life from birth to death is the task of the study of the development of religiosity," hinting that the study of religious development focuses on the psychological dimension of human beings. In addition, as Allport (1950) suggests, the development of religiosity is sometimes explained bearing "religious maturity" or "psychological maturity" in mind. Matsumoto (1979) also points out that the development of religiosity sometimes does not correspond to the process of aging (the role of age), and that there are cases where religiosity remains immature despite the individual becoming an adult, just as there are people who are religiously mature at a young age. However, in my study (Matsushima, 2011), the stages of aging, too, are found to be involved in the development of religiosity.

Furthermore, Hoshino (1977) describes the development of religious consciousness as follows:

Religious consciousness, just like consciousness concerning society and morals, develops from a simple, undifferentiated form to a highly complex and differentiated form in keeping with personal mental growth and religious influences and education, and transforms or collapses in response to the internal and external conditions of the individual. (p. 376)

According to Hoshino (1977), such characteristics can be observed from the differences in the stages of aging. Although there are problems with his approach in that he uses only Protestant teachings and thinking to build his model, let us next present his view.

Toddlerhood and early childhood are characterized by animistic and magical beliefs that spirits inhabit inorganic matter, as well as by holding and acting according to a literal belief in what their parents have told them. In late childhood, we see characteristics such as religious consciousness tinged with morality, as seen in the concepts of cause and effect or hell and heaven, as well as an inclination towards worldly benefits, such as praying in earnest when facing exams or illness in the family.

In adolescence, the ego develops, and young people begin to resist religious authority, dogmatic doctrine, and religious education. Experiencing inner conflict and anxiety towards life, adolescents seek a greater power to overcome these issues and sometimes awake to a new religious consciousness.

Thus, it is possible to think that religiosity is deeply related to the psychological development of the ego in the period from toddlerhood to adolescence, which precedes the journey of self-actualization, and that it undergoes developmental changes in relation to each stage.

Nonetheless, it is hard to think that religious maturity, as I mentioned earlier, can appear in the period from toddlerhood to childhood. While there might be individuals in whom it appears in adolescence, even these cases are extremely rare. Matsumoto too, argues about religious maturity in relation to the psychology of religion in adulthood. The same is true of self-actualization, which I think can be addressed in conjunction with the psychological development that occurs after individuals have reached adulthood, when the degree of their maturity changes substantially. Of course, there are individual differences as well, which will similarly exist during toddlerhood and adolescence. I believe that when we deal with religiosity, we also need to pay attention to these individual differences (I shall touch on the issue of individual differences in the next section, too).

Finally, I wish to point out something we need to be cautious about when studying the psychology of religion from a developmental perspective: what to regard as the development of religiosity (or the qualitative change in religiosity temporally) when conducting empirical research. Religious maturity and self-actualization may be the final (or, in a sense, the ultimate) destination as Allport (1950) and Matsumoto (1979) suggest, but it is not possible to conduct every study with that in mind. For that reason, when conducting empirical studies, we need to be mindful of the unique attributes of research participants. That is, in each study we have to think of development of religiosity for that particular sample who come with specific characteristics, and the characteristics of the participants' attributes will become clear during the process as well.

For example, in the study of the development of religiosity in Christianity (Matsushima, 2011), I recruited a sample of Japanese Christians whose unique attributes included being "a member of the Christian denomination A," "Japanese Christians," and "adolescents or adults." I created a developmental model of religiosity by examining the devotion to Christianity as an index of the developing ego. It is worth mentioning that the devotion to Christianity does not merely denote the deepening of beliefs, but the deepening of religiosity as a whole: knowledge, belief, experience, practice and effects.

This position situates the development of religiosity as a process related to self-actualization and attaches importance to the dimensions of the human mind and ego. That, however, does not mean that only the mind and consciousness are important. Rather, it implies that development (deepening or qualitative change) of human activity including experience and behavior is important as well.

To summarize, by addressing religiosity in developmental terms (temporally) we can capture its qualitative changes. To comprehend religiosity in more depth, it is extremely important that we approach it from the viewpoint of human development.

2.3 Addressing Religiosity as a Personal Trait

That we are able to address religiosity in developmental terms also means that, like sociability and morality, it can be treated as a trait possessed by humans (Hoshino, 1977). In other words, religiosity is a personal trait that everyone possesses, and can therefore be regarded as a concept for measuring human characteristics.

Upon seeing the phrase "religiosity is a personal trait that everyone possesses," more than a few readers may think, "I have no such thing as the trait of religiosity. Therefore, it cannot be that religiosity is a personal trait that all humans possess." It is, perhaps, those who self-identify is non-religious who feel that way most strongly. Nonetheless, think about sociability and morality. In everyday life we sometimes say that someone is "not sociable." It is probably because their social demeanor is very bad that they are described that way. But, that does not mean that we think sociability itself does not exist as a trait that all humans possess, does it? No, it probably just means that those who are described as "not sociable" have very little sociability. The same applies to our thinking regarding morality.

And the same goes for religiosity. Humans have much to do with matters regarding religion, and the fact that someone regards him- or herself as non-religious means that he or she lacks such awareness, which is different from religiosity itself not existing as a personal trait. And it is exactly because religiosity, too, is a personal trait, that individual variation exists; for example, person A is highly religious, whereas person

B is low in religiosity. These are the so-called "individual differences," and that is why we can say that there is variation among individuals in the way they engage in matters regarding religion, in how they inquire (knowledge), believe (belief), feel and experience (experience), act (practice), and how they are influenced (effects). For example, if we consider the kinds of things individuals desire (some prefer a religious group while others prefer spiritual things), individual differences in terms of the degree of preference for each of the domains will emerge.

Thus, when we treat religiosity as a personal trait that all human beings possess, individual differences become apparent, and religiosity becomes a functional concept that enables the measurement of human characteristics.

2.4 Studying Psychology of Religion is Possible

Religiosity exists as a notion for measuring human characteristics (individual traits). This means that religiosity, like sociability and morality, is nothing but a relative, operational criterion, which changes, depending on society, culture, and historical period. Therefore, I would like the readers to note that the notion of religiosity presented in this book by no means approaches the so-called "essence of religiosity" discussed in religious studies and elsewhere. Since traits cannot be measured if there is no standard for measurement, psychological research on religion is constructed by presenting the premise that religiosity is a personal trait that any human being possesses and therefore a notion that enables measuring human characteristics.

Thanks to the existence of that premise, we can grasp religiosity as individuals' traits with individual differences. Thus, we are able to capture religiosity quantitatively through psychological methods. Capturing religiosity quantitatively means being able to assign numeric values to individuals [4] (e.g., ten points to Mr. A, five points to Ms. B, etc.) followed by empirical interpretation of such data, which is the study of the psychology of religion.

Further, when we regard religiosity as an individual characteristic, the words the individual utters must have some unique significance regarding his or her religious views. There is a psychological approach of analyzing religiosity using personal statements as well. These personal accounts are called qualitative data, and the qualitative approach emphasizes the examination of those spoken words (i.e., narratives).

3. What to Pay Attention to When Studying the Psychology of Religion and Spirituality

In the previous section, I discussed the grounds for the possibility of the study of the psychology of religion using the notion of religiosity. In this section I wish to explain some of the issues in this field.

3.1 Understanding Religiosity as Human Activity

In section 2.3, I argued for addressing religiosity as a personal trait that any human being possesses, but treating religiosity as a personal trait also means treating it as a human activity. Similar to sociability and morality, religiosity is manifested in everyday life in the form of knowing, believing, feeling and experiencing, practicing, and being influenced by these, with regard to religious matters. In other words, religiosity is a human activity, and studying the psychology of religion involves strictly focusing on and examining human activity with scientific methodologies.

This act of pursuing the questions in matters regarding religion of how humans know, how they believe, how they feel and experience, how they practice and how they are influenced by these things, all from the perspective of human activity, is exactly what makes studying the psychology of religion what it is.[5]

Therefore, in the empirical psychological research of religion, we do not get involved in issues such as proving the existence of God or proving the existence of heaven and hell at all. These things do not pertain to human activities. However, we can deal with topics such as "how humans perceive God" or "how they feel His or Her presence." Such a research theme is not directed at proving the existence of God, but considers how humans think or feel about a being called "God," and deals with the problem of human cognition and emotion.

Psychology is an academic discipline that approaches physical living beings, especially humans in this real world. Thus, empirical psychological research of religion also takes that stance, and is a field that approaches only those study objects that can be treated as human activity (i.e., religiosity).

3.2 Strictness of Study Procedure

Whether the research is quantitative or qualitative, research procedures need to be implemented strictly. What procedures to use and how to implement the study—the participants, time and method, ethical considerations, composition of the questions (scales), data analysis, etc.—should all be sufficiently and carefully examined. It goes without saying that, to be able to do so, it is necessary to formulate in advance a thorough research plan. Based on such a plan, we proceed to create as rigorously as possible a design concerning how to implement the study and what research method to use. It is precisely this procedural rigor that is a *sine qua non* for conducting empirical research. And by scrupulously describing that procedure and publishing it, we demonstrate the soundness of the procedure.

3.3 Strictness of Research Methodology

Strictness in the research methodology, too, is a necessity. In psychology, numerous introductory and explanatory books have been published regarding research methodology. Making sure that our research procedure is rigorous enables us to maintain the standards of empirical research. Therefore, when taking a psychological approach, dealing with the study method is essential.

Naturally, the same is required when studying the psychology of religion. In psychological studies problems exist, such as sampling, the validity of the data (how accurately the traits one wants to measure have been captured) and reliability (how consistent or stable the measurements are).[6] How these problems should be solved has been debated in numerous empirical research projects in various ways. Nonetheless, what is important is to conduct research as rigorously as possible including its procedures. Thus, when studying the psychology of religion, methodological rigor should under no circumstances be sidestepped either.

4. An Invitation to the Psychology of Religion and Spirituality

Since we argue that religiosity is a personal trait that all humans possess, regardless of cultural context, it is possible to study the psychology of religion. However, since religion depends heavily on society and culture (Kaneko, 1997), not taking such considerations into account would mean missing the point. The same can be said of religious groups. When investigating a certain religion (through the people involved in it), thorough research cannot be done without examining the historical background in which that religion was born. That is, studying the psychology of religion requires two aspects: an approach to participants themselves (their personal traits), and an approach to the collective, the society and culture in which those participants are embedded.

Unfortunately, empirical psychological research on religion taking the Japanese as participants has not been vigorous until now (Matsushima, 2012). Precisely because religion is heavily dependent on society and culture, Japanese possess a uniquely Japanese religiosity, and the need exists to conduct analyses and investigation based on empirical data from the Japanese context.

Knowing religion translates to knowing humans, knowing society, knowing Japan, and knowing the world. If we do not understand religion, we cannot understand human beings, society, Japan or the world. This book presents religion as an activity of humans, with the special case of the Japanese social situation. Through this book, I hope that the readers learn about our approach to the study of the psychology of religion and spirituality and sense its potential.

Notes:

[1] Table 1 was made by Nishiwaki (2004), who, having analyzed several previously conducted international and domestic surveys, summarized the characteristics of the religiosity of the contemporary Japanese. Although the table was created in 2004, a glance at the results of the NHK survey conducted in 2013 (NHK Broadcasting Culture Research Institute, 2015) and the Asahi Newspaper survey conducted in 2015 (Sawada, 2015) suggests almost identical trends as in the characteristics of religiosity of the Japanese summarized by Nishiwaki (2004).

[2] "Matters regarding religion" here includes both what the people themselves perceive as such, and what others perceive as such even if those people themselves do not. It is as the proverb "even sardine heads have value to those who have faith in them" says, and the understanding of what matters regarding religion does differ greatly from person to person and reflects personal thinking and values. Moreover, it often happens that even though a person claims that something has nothing to do with religion, those around that person think it does. Bearing these situations in mind, I have opted for the above view of "matters regarding religion."

³ Hori (1991) demonstrates that actual human development unfolds with the three aspects intertwined. The same applies to the development of religiosity, but it may be said that in it, the most prominent aspect is "Development as self-actualization."

⁴ Rules for assigning points, such as 1 point in this case or 3 points in that case, are what is generally called "a scale," while the process of allotting numerical values to study participants, such as person A or person B., etc, is called "measurement" (Haebara, 2011).

⁵ Scientific psychology, including the empirical psychology of religion, takes as its object of study, solely (the activities of) living physical beings, including humans.

⁶ While I wish to leave a more detailed argument for a future paper, I will just briefly mention that various arguments have been put forth in psychology about what being scientific, empirical, or objective means. Also, since in this book I have not been able to concretely bring this issue up, regarding the treatment of study methods in psychology of religion, I would like the readers to refer to Matsushima (2014). About psychological methodology in general, see Haebara, Ichikawa and Shimoyama (2001); Takano and Oka (2004) and Murai (2012).

1.

Exploring Japanese Religiosity after the Great East Japan Earthquake of 2011: Memorializing Tragic Deaths of Children

Tetsuo Ohmura, Tohoku University

1. Introduction

In this chapter, I will explore the implicit psychological meaning behind people's non-rational behavior (phenomena). After the Great East Japan Earthquake of 2011 (Figure 1.1), I first noticed that deceased children were receiving diplomas. It is an unusual practice, and quite inconsistent with the pragmatic way of thinking that we are all used to. Although there have been some anecdotes of this sort here and there around the country, the massive scale of such a practice was certainly unheard of. Who initiates this and why do they do it? Is this a common practice that people rarely talk about? Does it help the surviving families to accept the untimely deaths of their children? What is the relationship between this practice and the religious beliefs in Japan?

I will present the result of my study based on survey responses from the schools that were affected by the Earthquake. Furthermore, I will compare the practice of awarding posthumous diplomas and other memorization practices for deceased children, and analyze the meaning of the awards from the surviving family members' perspective. Finally, I will explore similar beliefs and practices around the world in which the deceased becomes a sacred and protective being for the surviving family. My findings are that such non-rational thinking and practices are universal and intertwine with people's religious beliefs, and they eventually help the surviving family regain some peace of mind.

Figure 1.1 *Okawa Elementary School, Ishinomaki (70 deaths and 4 missing students were reported after the Great East Japan Earthquake of 2011). Photo by Tetsuo Ohmura*

2. Spring in the Disaster Area – Diplomas for the Deceased

The Great East Japan Earthquake occurred on March 11, 2011. It happened during the junior high school graduation period that followed the high school graduation period in the region. Elementary school graduation ceremonies were yet to be held. Inevitably, many were canceled that year. During the graduation season for the next couple of years, media reported that diplomas were given to the deceased children, who were the victims of the earthquake. Such a practice is not unheard of. In fact, there were previous reports of granting diplomas to children who died due to illness, accidents, suicide (often because of bullying), etc.; however, this was never a topic of scientific investigation. In the following section, I will examine how people dealt with the untimely deaths of many children due to the earthquake and how people tried to cope with it. In particular, the focus will be on awarding posthumous diplomas, and the role that Japanese religious beliefs played in the context of public schools, where a strict demarcation of state and religion is generally drawn.

3. Japanese Religiosity and Memorial Services at Public School
3.1 Japanese Religiosity

Japanese are often said to be non-religious. However, this does not mean that they lack religiosity. For example, according to *Yomiuri* Newspaper's (2008) nation-wide survey, while 71.9% of Japanese self-reported that they did not have any religious faith, 78.3% regularly visited their family cemetery during Buddhist holidays, and 73.1% visited *Shinto* shrines and or Buddhist temples in the New Year. Further, people believed that the soul of the deceased reincarnate (29.8%), move on to the other side (23.8%), and remain in the cemetery (9.9%), suggesting their belief in eternal souls.

Such complex psychological characteristics among Japanese should not be described in a religious/non-religious or faith/non-faith dichotomy. Instead I use religiosity to refer to characteristics that are the backbone of our religious psyche even if a person denies that he or she is religious. Thus, I define religiosity as "a non-rational attitude or meaning-making stance with regard to any phenomena either within the self or between the self and the outer world, that are beyond one's control" (Ohmura, 2010). Although spirituality is a similar concept, it often carries a positive connotation (e.g., concerning the meaning of life) and may not be appropriate for a Japanese religious psyche that has a more ambiguous nuance that incorporates views on nature and life/death. In addition to the awe that Japanese feel toward divine beings, the affinity that they feel for all "things," either natural (e.g., mountains, forests, boulders, ancient trees, rivers, the ocean, animals, and plants) or artificial objects, is an indispensable component of Japanese religiosity.

See Figure 1.2, for example. There are a number of versions of *Hyakki Yagyo* scroll ("Night Parade of One Hundred Demons"), but the original is said to have been painted before the *Muromachi* period (14th Century). It is a humorous painting based on quite a simple story that lots of "things" become demons and parade until dawn. The belief at the time seemed to assume that even inanimate objects such as pots and pans possessed souls or spirits. The fact that people used the same motif over the centuries in different paintings indicates that Japanese religiosity incorporates the idea that all things possess souls or spirits.

Figure 1.2 *Hyakki Yagyo scroll (Night Parade of One Hundred Demons, 16th cent).* Tohoku University Library

3.2 Public School and Memorial Services

The Japanese Constitution Article 20.3 states that "The State and its organs shall refrain from religious education or any other religious activity." Thus, any religious activity is prohibited at Japanese public schools. Similarly, the Basic Act of Education Article 15.2 states that "The schools established by the national and local governments shall refrain from religious education in favor of any specific religion, and from other religious activities." Accordingly, upon the death of a student, public schools are only allowed to hold a secular gathering without any religious overtones, and they may not conduct a funeral or religious service that memorializes the "soul" of the deceased. This strict rule is due to the lesson learned from the abuse of *Shinto* ideology by the pre-war imperial government. However, psychological care and support, such as sending clinical psychologists to schools, do not seem to be enough in the case of tragic deaths of small children. The rational and scientific approach of psychotherapy was only able to support the "lives" of the survivors, but failed to resolve their non-material issues such as concern for the souls of the deceased and the after world.

3.3 Posthumous Diploma in Lieu of Religious Care

Before I discuss the awarding of posthumous diplomas for the purpose of memorializing the deceased children in public school settings, I would like to clarify what we mean by diploma. A diploma certifies that a promotion has been conferred to an individual who has completed the required classes/courses. According to the Ordinance for Enforcement of the School Education Act (Ministry of Education Ordinance 11), "A principal must deliver a diploma to elementary students who have completed all required curricula." Article 58 includes junior highs, high schools, special support schools, and universities which must give diplomas (a public document) to those who completed the curriculum. Therefore, awarding a diploma to a deceased child who is no longer a member of the school is technically an illegal act. I argue that the prevalence of such a practice is indicative of its enormous benefit over the obvious disadvantage (i.e., the violation of law), and that its function is to substitute for religion at public schools in order to memorialize the souls of the deceased and comfort the survivors.

4. Empirical Study
4.1 Participants

This is an on-going study covering three prefectures affected by the Great East Japan Earthquake (Fukushima, Miyagi, and Iwate). Here, I report data from 2013 and 2016 in Miyagi Prefecture. There were a total of 327 deaths at 95 schools with 35 still missing: eight deaths at three kindergartens (1 missing), 167 deaths at 33 elementary schools (19 missing), 66 deaths at 22 junior high schools, 79 deaths at 35 high schools (8 missing), and 5 deaths at 2 special support schools (Miyagi Prefectural Board of Education, 2013). This study includes all the schools and kindergartens where at least one student has died.

4.2 Methods

Semi-structured questionnaires were mailed to principals of the respective schools in early April in 2012 and 2016, and data collection was completed each year at the end of that month.

4.3 Questions

1) Whether or not, between 2011 and 2016, there were graduation ceremonies for grades in which at least one student had passed away or was missing

2) Whether or not diplomas were given to the deceased or missing students

3) Diploma format (Was the diploma format the same as those given to the other students?)

4) Ceremony format (Was the diploma awarding ceremony format the same as that for the other students?)

5) Who came up with the idea of awarding posthumous diplomas and why? (Answer choices were teachers, including the principal and vice principal, family members of the deceased students, family members of other students, the local board of education, the regional board of education, etc.)

6) Whether they had any precedents of awarding posthumous diplomas

7) Open-ended comments

I paid extremely close attention to the wording of these questions to avoid being invasive by making it clear that they did not have to answer questions if they did not wish to. I also stated explicitly in the cover letter and the survey itself that I was not being judgmental about the practice of posthumous diploma awarding.

5. Results and Discussion
5.1 Response Rates

The response rates for data collection combined for kindergartens, elementary schools, junior high schools, high schools, and special support schools are, respectively, 66.7%, 60.6%, 86.4%, 74.3%, and 100%, with the average of 72.6%. Given the sensitive nature of this investigation (e.g., the legality of awarding posthumous diplomas, the possible liabilities for schools, etc.) coupled with the fact that some schools were permanently closed or merged after the earthquake, the response rates are quite impressive. I also received information that the diplomas were given posthumously at several schools that did not respond to my investigation.

5.2 Awarding Posthumous Diplomas

The rates of awarding posthumous diplomas are presented in Table 1.1. The practice was common among kindergartens, elementary, junior high schools, and high schools but no diplomas were awarded at special support schools. Could it be that the need to "present the diploma" was stronger for the lower grade schools, since they are mostly operated by local (i.e., town, village, and city) governments and thus have closer ties to the communities than high schools and special support schools?

Table 1.1 The Rates of Awarding Posthumous Diplomas

Educational establishment	Kindergartens	Elementary schools	Junior high schools	High schools	Special support schools
The rate of awarding	66.7%	33.3%	59.1%	2.9%	0%

5.3 Years of the Commencement Ceremony

The number of students and years of the commencement ceremonies where diplomas were handed out posthumously are presented in Table 1.2. Note that diplomas were given posthumously not only on the year of the earthquake but also in subsequent years in 2012, 2013, 2015, and 2016. This finding indicates that the deceased students "advanced" to higher grades and "graduated" with the rest of the students.

Table 1.2 Number of Students and Year of the Commencement Ceremonies Where Diplomas Were Awarded Posthumously

	Kindergartens	Elementary schools	Junior high schools	High schools	Total
2011	1	2	5	–	8
2012	0	4	20	1	25
2013	1	10	11	0	22
2014	0	0	0	0	0
2015	0	1	0	0	1
2016	0	1	0	0	1

Note. Some elementary/junior high school graduation ceremonies were canceled in 2011 because of the Great East Japan Earthquake. There were no high schools that diplomas were given to the deceased children because graduation ceremonies had already been held before the earthquake.

5.4 Format of the Posthumous Diplomas

While one junior high school reported that they used the same diploma format as that of the rest of the students, all other schools did not include the "graduation numbers," which must be recorded on the official "graduation registry" of each school. In other words, it is an ambiguous practice in which the diploma is treated as a private document and not a public document, as it legally should be.

5.5 The Originator of the Idea of Awarding Posthumous Diplomas

Who came up with the idea of posthumous diploma awarding? Were they the surviving family members or the teachers? All schools reported that it was the idea of the teachers who empathized with the surviving families. Somehow, the schools felt it was imperative to memorialize the deceased students.

5.6 Rationale for Awarding Posthumous Diplomas

The following are open-ended responses regarding the rationale for posthumous awarding diplomas.

> A) Kindergartens
> *The parents were grieving after having lost three of five family members (an aging mother and two young children). They regularly came to our events (e.g., athletic day, presentations, etc.) even after the earthquake because they said they could feel the presence of their children. All of us were dispirited for those two years. We came up with the diploma idea because we empathized with the parents who didn't want people to forget their children. We presented the diploma as a proof that these children did live and spend time together with us.*
>
> *They were once alive. We lived and shared the same space and time, and we just wanted to value that experience.*

It was the result of both sympathy for the parents and the desires of teachers.

> B) Elementary schools
> *We discussed among ourselves about what other schools were doing. The guardians (i.e., grandparents because the parents were also killed in tsunami) expressed an interest in participating in the graduation ceremony. We gave them the diplomas in the cer-*

emony after everyone else.

Because the guardians and the teachers all agreed to do it.
To respect the feelings of the surviving guardians.

Because of the requests by the families of the graduating students.

They were all students of ours. That fact remains unchanged.

To memorialize the deceased.

As sympathy to the surviving family members.

As an expression of school's attitude that we would never forget these children.

The decision was based on the feelings of the surviving families, the teachers' ideas, and a prayer for the deceased children.

C) Junior high schools
The principal deemed them to have completed all the required curriculum.

The principal came up with the idea because 1) The students died while under our supervision, and they were all supposed to graduate together; 2) We asked the surviving families about the diploma, and they welcomed our idea; 3) These deceased students along with those who moved after the disaster always wanted to graduate together.

The teachers and the guardians of the other students came up with the idea because they all wanted to graduate together.

The principal and the local board of education came up with the idea to celebrate the graduation for the deceased and living students.

The principal, the teachers, and the students collectively came up with the idea that the diplomas should be given as a proof that they were a part of our school.

Upon the request by the principal and the students, we decided to do this to show our sympathy to the surviving grandparents and to pay respect to the deceased classmates.

Our principal proposed the ceremony after receiving many requests from the guardians and surviving families.
The teachers came up with the idea in response to the requests from the guardians.

The vice-principal and the teachers came up with the idea to sympathize with the surviving family members.

The idea of awarding posthumous diplomas came from the surviving families, the teachers, and the guardians of other families.

5.7 The Decision to Not Award Diplomas Posthumously

There were several schools that did not give diplomas posthumously. The following narratives reveal both explicit and implicit reasons.

A) Elementary schools
There was no one left in the family to receive the diploma because they all died in the disaster. We decided not to give the diploma posthumously because that might upset their classmates.

The guardians had already moved to another prefecture.

There have been several arguments reported elsewhere that the subject of "death" should not be brought up because it may upset the children. There seems to be two opposing camps regarding this argument when the children actually face the deaths of their classmates.

B) Junior high schools
We did not promote the deceased students to the senior year; No requests were made by the guardians; We plan to erect a memori-

al monument and hold an annual memorial service instead.

We did not give the diplomas posthumously in 2012, because everything was still too chaotic after only one year. Although several students died who were not under our supervision, everyone at the graduation felt reluctant to accept the tragedy as a group. However, we did ask the surviving families to attend the ceremony, and presented the yearbook to them (we gave diplomas posthumously in 2013).

Erecting a monument and planning for an annual ceremony in the future are a part of memorializing (religious) effort by a public school. Also, the fact that the school officials, who actually dealt with the deaths of these students, were still suffering psychological pain even one year after the disaster suggests the magnitude of this tragedy.

C) High schools

Several high schools reported that they acted strictly based on the rule that the children would lose their student status at the time of death. In addition, a few reported that the decision of not awarding diplomas posthumously was based on the schools' speculation about the feelings of the surviving families. This speculation and subsequent inaction are the total opposite of those made by the lower grade, mandatory schools. However, one high school that had a precedent of this practice did consider giving a diploma, but decided not to because in this case they speculated that such an action might disturb the feelings of the surviving family members. Having precedents seemed to encourage the option of this practice.

D) Special support schools

He/she was not a graduate.

It simply states that the deceased child was not regarded as a graduate.

5.8 Methods of Diploma Delivery

There were several ways that school delivered the diploma posthumously. For example, they handed out the diploma to the surviving siblings and parents or to the valedictorian during the commencement. In other cases, school officials gave the diploma to the surviving family members or the guardians on different occasions. Various methods of delivery were selected as a result of the discussion between the school and the surviving family.

5.9 Influence of Precedents for Awarding Posthumous Diplomas

I found that all levels of schools, except the special support schools, had precedents for awarding posthumous diplomas. A total of 11 out of 13 kindergartens, elementary, and junior high schools mentioned above had presented posthumous diplomas to students who died due to illnesses, accidents, and crimes. Several reported that their decision was influenced by media reports of such phenomena at other schools after the quake.

5.10 Summary

1) Kindergartens (66.7%), elementary schools (33.3%), junior high (59.1%), and high schools (2.9%) gave out diplomas posthumously, but no special support schools did.
2) The idea of presenting posthumous diplomas was often initiated by schools that accepted requests from other students and their parents. In other words, in addition to the surviving families, there seemed to be psychological needs to carry out this ceremony among other students and their teachers and parents.
3) Posthumous diplomas were often given in subsequent years when the victims' cohorts were graduating. This fact suggests that people shared the idea of deceased moving up to higher grades with other students until graduation. This idea is consistent with the folk belief/practice of "counting the age of a deceased child."
4) No graduation registry numbers were printed on the posthumous diplomas. This practice reflects its ambiguous nature that it is regarded as something in between public and private. This alone symbolizes that the act of issuing the diploma is an act of private mourning conducted at schools, and other public venues, where conducting religious activities is forbidden.
5) Precedents and knowledge of such practices through mass media increased the likelihood of engaging in the posthumous awarding of diplomas.

6. Memorializing Children: A Comparison with Folk Practices

If still alive, my son/daughter would have been graduating this year.

He/she would have been in school by now walking under these blossoming cherry trees.

These are common sentiments among parents who lost their young children. While all deaths are tragic, the deaths of young children are especially painful, and these feelings may be the foundation of a folk practice that memorializes deceased children.

Figure 1.3 *Kawakura Jizo Hall. Photo by Tetsuo Ohmura*

Figure 1.3 depicts the Kawakura *Jizo* (the Buddhist deity of children) Hall in Kanagi-machi, Aomori Prefecture. Around a large stone statue of *Jizo* stand numerous small ones that have been donated by families who lost their young children. They wear make-up and traditional items such as straw sandals and cotton towels, as well as more contemporary items including school supplies, backpacks, toys, shoes, and snacks. I have been visiting this hall every year with my students and noticed that these items have been replaced by new ones, indicating frequent visits by the family members. We always become speechless in the presence of countless *Jizo* and the items decorating them in this relatively large space. It may be the painful yearning of the surviving parents or the presence of the wandering souls of the children. Whatever it is, this place is always suffocating to us.

Figure 1.4 *Kawakura Jizo. Photo by Tetsuo Ohmura*

At this hall, *Jizo* is the primary object of worship (Figure 1.4). This Buddhist deity not only represents each of the deceased children but also is regarded as a guardian who saves the suffering souls of children by the river that separates the material world and the after world. This *Jizo* worship is not confined to the Tohoku region but is expressed in different types of *Jizo* found around the nation including those that represent miscarried and aborted fetuses and the victims of traffic accidents, the *Six Jizo* at Buddhist cemeteries, and the stone *Jizo* found at the perimeter of houses and temples. These *Jizo* are the expression of our collective yearning for our deceased children which has remained the same over the centuries; Jizo's appearance has changed from the stern look of *samurai* warriors in the Middle Ages to a more contemporary, caring look of a protector. In addition, the traditional *Jizo* usually wears a Buddhist stole around its neck, but over the years, people, especially in the Western part of Japan, began to put on a bib instead. In a sense, *Jizo* worship became the primary outlet for the surviving parents' yearning and regrets, and the guardian deity of children and the deceased children have become one.

There is another memorial section at Kawakura *Jizo* Hall. Behind the *Jizo* for miscarried and aborted fetuses, there are numerous traditional Japanese dolls in glass cases (Figure 1.5). These are called "Bride Dolls" or "Groom Dolls" for those children who passed away before they had the chance to get married. They were donated by the surviving families at the time their children reached the "appropriate age" had they still been alive. They are in pairs, and the "partner" usually has a specific name.

Figure 1.5 *A Bride Doll at Kawakura Jizo. Photo by Tetsuo Ohmura*

The idea of "the marriage of the deceased" is quite strange for people in a contemporary society, but this practice is not that unusual. It is a well-known fact that there are many "Bride Dolls" displayed in the *Yasukuni* Shrine in Tokyo (where fallen soldiers are worshiped). It suggests that we can empathize with the regrets and misfortunes that the deceased must have experienced. This practice is also known as "posthumous marriage," and other instances are reported across cultures. Unlike the belief system in the past, we may no longer think that there is an afterworld where the deceased are still "living," but the simple idea that "the deceased children age as we all do" is not so incompatible with our rational thoughts.

Getting back to the topic of posthumous diplomas, there are such numerous instances around the nation that the practice has already become a folk tradition. Examples include: three students of Kyoto University lost in the Great East Japan Earthquake (Kyoto University Newspaper, 2011), high school students lost in a mud slide in Hiroshima on March 1, 2015 (NHK news), a high school student lost in a traffic accident a few days later (Kagoshima Yomiuri TV), a high school student who died of natural causes in Hokkaido on March 6, 2015 (Tokachi Mainichi Shinbun News), and an elementary school child receiving a diploma six years after death on March 26, 2015 (Kobe Shinbun NEXT).

Is this practice unique to Japan? I am currently collaborating with researchers abroad and finding out that that is not the case. For example, I found an example of posthumous diploma presented to a high school student who died in a hurricane in the U.S. This practice may be an effective ritual that not only consoles the surviving families but also memorializes the deceased. It is not exactly a "religious" practice, but it certainly deals with the "religiosity" of the people involved.

7. What is Memorialization?

I found that the motivation to memorialize the deceased among the survivors of the earthquake was a sense of regret that "the person who died wasn't me, but you." Survivors of the small children must have held an extreme sense of regret. This accentuated "survivor's guilt" along with the notion that the deceased souls are still suffering in limbo, makes it difficult for the family members to move on with their lives. People also memorialize the soul of the deceased not only to mitigate feelings such as grudges and envy that the souls may still hold, but also to make these souls the protectors of the survivors. For example, *Suitengu* (the shrines for the God of Water) is worshiped as the god who protects people from water-related accidents, as well as for healthy pregnancy. This god is believed to have originated from a young Emperor *Antoku* who drowned in *Dan-no-ura* during the *Genpei* War in the 1180s. As he was memorialized over the centuries, he became sanctified as the God of Water. More recently, a policeman who contracted cholera about 120 years ago was eventually sanctified to become the God of Police, worshiped for its power over public health and academic performances (*Masuda Shinto* Shrine in Saga Prefecture) (Nishimura, 2013).

By the same token, Christians worship many protective saints. The common practice of naming children after the saints, such as *St. George*, *St. Clare*, and *St. Mary*, is indicative of this tradition. In particular, people believe that if the saints were Christian martyrs, they have special power. For example, *St. Lucia* in the 4th Century was tortured by eye-gouging, and as a result, she became the patron saint of eye diseases. This is why *St. Lucy* is often depicted in paintings as holding two eyes on a plate (see Figure. 1.6). Further, to honor this saint in Northern Europe, a young girl dressed in white with a crown of candles on her head performs a procession around the time of Winter Solstice to celebrate the return of Light. Similarly, in the 3rd Century *St. Apollonia* was tortured by having her teeth pulled out and became a patron saint of dentistry. She is often portrayed with a pair of pliers (Figure. 1.7). *St. Agatha* was also martyred

Figure 1.6 *St. Lucia (Domenico Beccafumi, 1521). Pinacoteca Nazionale*

Figure 1.7 *St. Apollonia (Francisco de Zurbarian, 1636). Louvre Museum*

Figure 1.8 *St. Agatha (Francisco de Zurbarian, 1630-33). Musse Fabre*

after torture involving the severing of her breasts. She eventually became a patron saint of bell founders, as she is often depicted holding a tray with breasts that look like bells (Figure 1.8).

There are many instances in which a martyr becomes a guardian or protector. Christ is a good example; his torture instrument, the cross, came to symbolize salvation. We seem to believe that memorializing rituals calm the souls of deceased children or people with a pure and innocent heart. By elevating the status of such people to a protector, our sense of survivor's guilt seems to diminish.

What does it really mean to memorialize the deceased (i.e., consoling their souls)? Must one presume that souls exist? Komatsu (2002) hypothesizes that "the soul of the deceased is a type of 'memory device' that stores memories of the deceased" (p. 110). In other words, the practice of consoling souls does not necessarily presume the existence of the soul or an afterworld but can be interpreted as a type of cognitive device compatible with contemporary rationality. Komatsu continues, "by repeating the ritual of consoling the 'soul' of the deceased, the surviving family members are eventually freed from a sense of guilt and regret" (p. 113). I agree with these points, but I disagree with Komatsu in what he says next: "The soul as a memory device was necessarily generated by the sentiment of the survivors who were struggling to preserve such memories" (p. 104). Instead, I argue that we perform memorial rituals in order to forget the deceased. I believe that the memorial service provides an opportunity for the survivors to remember for one day, so that for the rest of the year they could bury the tragedy in oblivion.

In short, the memorialization is a ritual that has two opposing sides, memory and oblivion. In the *Kangin-shu*, a collection of informal poetry form 1518, a short poem seems to express this sentiment. "The fact you remember me now means that you had forgotten about me. If you hadn't forgotten about me, there would be no need to remember me" (p. 85). The poem suggests that while one is infatuated with and constantly thinking about a lover, he or she is not able to do other things. The person is only able to deal with his or her life once again, after being able both to forget and to remember the lover. In other words, we memorialize to forget and to live. By doing so, the surviving families can console the souls of the deceased and live their own lives.

8. Conclusion

In this chapter, I explored the meaning of awarding posthumous diplomas. It is quite non-rational for public schools to engage in such a practice in which the deceased are memorialized and eventually elevated to a status of protector or guardian angel; however, there are numerous examples of this not only in Tohoku but also in other parts of Japan and the world. These findings suggest that the memorialization is not based on rationality but rather, that this is necessary for human beings across different cultures. When people engage in non-rational behavior (e.g., athletes performing ritual routines) psychological reasons always exist.

There has been quite a lot of talk about the uselessness of religious rituals and monuments, including funerals and cemeteries. In fact, 80% of

Japanese claim they are non-religious, and an increasing number of them opt for "direct burial" and ash scattering without any religious ceremonies. On the other hand, a large majority of funerals are conducted following the Buddhist tradition. This discrepancy suggests that the funeral ceremonies are no longer religious but merely a cultural practice, and that cultural practice is a necessary outlet for the surviving families. Similarly, memorialization is non-rational yet meaningful. It gives an opportunity for people to remember the deceased in order to forget, which allows the survivors to move on with their lives. Further, the deceased often becomes the protector of the survivors, and such a non-rational "system" may be necessary for people to accept the death of the loved ones. I think exploring such phenomena is what "psychologizing religion" really means.

2.

Role of Religion in the Aftermath of a Major Disaster: A Lesson from the Great Hanshin-Awaji Earthquake

Daisuke Kawashima, Chukyo University
Yu Urata, Osaka University

1. Introduction

Tragic disasters change many lives. As we write this article in April 2016, the Kumamoto Earthquake has hit the land, and many have been affected by it. The Great East Japan Earthquake in 2011, the so-called 3.11 Earthquake, and the tsunami also have left tremendous scars both on people's hearts as well as on the land. As of now, over 170,000 people are still forced to live in shelters while their lives are continually under threat. Perhaps the complication with the nuclear reactor meltdown makes the event especially unforgettable. It is no surprise that the memories from these two events are still fresh and vivid due to their recency.

Japanese people experienced many natural disasters in the past, and some say that the Great Hanshin-Awaji Earthquake that occurred in 1995 has faded away from people's memories. However, especially for those who lost their loved ones, the Great Hanshin-Awaji Earthquake continues to impact their lives even 20 years after the event. Though the extent of the impact from the earthquake may vary from person to person, religion has played a significant role in the course of grieving and recovery.

The occurrence and significance of the relief care by religious professionals have been catching people's attention, especially after the 3.11

earthquake (Fujimaru, 2013; Kitamura, 2013). In fact, there has been an ongoing debate about the role that religion plays in the aftermath of 3.11, featuring many different perspectives in a journal published by the International Institute for the Study of Religions (2013). However, this is a rather new trend. During the aftermath of the Great Hanshin-Awaji Earthquake, many volunteer teams were formed and sent by religious groups, and greatly contributed to the relief care by serving hot meals and offering listening ears (IISR, 1996). Further, people of faith put great effort as non-religious volunteers in an attempt to heal wounded hearts; however, such effort and their contribution had gone rather unnoticed (Miki, 2001).

There is only limited work in Japan on the topic of religion and the impact of natural disasters, let alone psychological studies that investigate how religion functions in people's experience of loss and grief that follow. As a result, little is known of what kind of long-term role religion plays in disaster relief care in Japan (Urata, 2014). How does religion help support those who lost everything they had including their houses and family members to disasters? What role does religion play in people's long journey of grief and healing? Those are the questions that have never been answered. The purpose of this study is to investigate this very question through qualitative research, which allows us to capture rich narratives that are rooted in individuals' unique views and in their experiences.

2. Background and Fieldwork
2.1 Background

This study is composed of ethnographic observations and in-depth, semi-structured interviews in the community surrounding the memorial monument of the Great Hanshin-Awaji Earthquake, as well as a literature search on this topic (NPO organization, 2004). The monument is situated in the area of Kobe City that had the most severe fire damage. When we visited its 20th anniversary event, the annual Buddhist Memorial Candle Service especially caught our attention. What makes this event very interesting is the cooperation among *Soto* monk volunteers gathered from all over Japan, local non-profit organizations, and local residents as well.

In the park where the Buddhist Memorial Candle Service takes place, there is a burnt, tilted utility pole that is purposely left untouched as a reminder of the disaster. Engraved with the words "Rest in Peace," the stone monument covered with flowers tells stories of the past, commemorating the lost and the bereaved. While this particular corner of the park remains important to those who live in the area, it is also a place where children and young families gather and play. The contrast between the past and the present is also evident in how the neighboring areas are divided. The severely damaged areas have been readjusted into town-lots with new buildings. The remaining area, which is just a block away with many narrow streets, still carries the old downtown feel and provides a vivid impression of what that area used to look like in the past.

In the following account, we will first introduce the Buddhist Memorial Candle Service by sharing the field notes from the ethnographic observation carried out at this location over a number of hours from February of 2013 to January of 2015. The interviews of the event organizers, a *Soto* monk and the head of a non-profit organization, and two sets of bereaved families reveal the impact this event had on people's lives and their meaning-making processes from their own unique perspectives. The semi-structured interviews using an interview guide were conducted from June of 2013 to May of 2014 (Figure 2.1 and Figure 2.2).

2.2. Field Notes from the Buddhist Memorial Candle Service

In early morning before dawn, we arrived at the park in Kobe City. The temperature was low, but not low enough to freeze our fingers. The sky was clear with a slightly waning moon and a few shining stars. Upon our arrival, we saw about 100 candles, all lit and placed around the monument. Firewood set inside two oil drums was lit. It was still far from dawn; candles were the only source of light illuminating the monument.

The fire started burning with vigor. There were some twenty people who looked like journalists and camera crews or staff, setting up their gadgets and preparing for the event.

It was not until a little later that people started gathering. Three girls who looked to be in their early teens cheerfully walked into the park from the west, followed by a couple of families with children, and a group of middle-aged people who seemed to know each other arrived from the north side while from the east side, about 10 middle-aged and older people walked into the park. The clock struck 10 minutes before the time the earthquake hit. The conversation we overheard between a middle-aged woman and a journalist who was taking notes while listening to her talk went like this: "No, none of my family died. But I lost one of my neighbors that we were close to…" There were three to four other journalists who having similar conversations.

Turning our eyes to the corner of the park at the back of the stone monument, we noticed that there was a photograph of a deceased person right by the playground. It appeared to be a picture of a young woman and was placed alongside a candle, a flower and incense burning on a stand. Although it was rather unclear how old she was due to the darkness, a woman with a surgical mask came by, placed an incense stick, and prayed. I approached her and asked if I could do the same. "Yes, please. Thank you," she said. While I brought out a Buddhist rosary and prayed, thoughts like "Should I start a conversation with this person to find out more about her?" or "I wonder if this young woman is her daughter" arose. I ended up not initiating a conversation because the ceremony was about to start, and so left the site after bowing to the woman. A group of young girls who were standing close to the bonfire noticed the photograph shortly after and put their heads together; they seemed to be discussing whether or not they should join their hands in prayer. They eventually turned their bodies towards the stone monument, rather uncomfortably, while a few other people went on to put their hands together in prayer in front of the photograph.

After the clock struck 5:40 a.m., a few monks dressed in clerical garments started walking towards the monument. "Please keep quiet; the ceremony is about to start." The announcement was made to the group that had grown to about 50 to 60 people by this time. About 70% of them were gathering close to the stone monument, while the rest remained standing around the bonfire towards the back. The woman I saw earlier was standing away from the playground, setting the photograph in front of her alongside a man who looked to be her husband. The monks stood around the monument, facing the participants. A time signal from a radio let us know that the time was upon us. "Let's pray in silence," a monk said.

After a minute of silent prayer, the monks started recit-

Figure 2.1 *Annual Buddhist Memorial Candle Service. Photo by Yu Yrata*

Figure 2.2 *Memorial Monument of the Great Hanshin-Awaji Earthquake. Photo by Daisuke Kawashima*

ing Hannya-Shingyo (Heart Sutra) solemnly. As we listened to them chant, which was low-pitched and traveled very well in the cold air, the announcement was made that people could start lining up in pairs to light incense. In order to show respect and be considerate to the locals, I stayed back and watched everyone go first. When I looked back, the couple who set the photograph in front of them were distancing themselves from the rest of the group, simply standing and watching the crowd.

As I was making my way back after lighting incense, I realized how cold it had become. I thought to myself, "Was it this cold on the day people were thrown out of their houses and buried underneath the buildings?" A middle-aged woman came close to the group of men and women standing in front of us and asked where her friend was. Somebody from the group answered, saying that she had been here for a while now. People there seemed to know each other. I recognized one of them—she was the one who had been interviewed. The woman looked up at the sky and shouted, "Mr. B, Mrs. C, do you see us? Mrs. D, can you see us? Mr. E, are you here with us?" The monks' chants continued in the background. A group of women around her stayed quiet, watching the ceremony proceed.

The couple with the photograph went last, bowed to the monks and placed their incense. Then it was finally monks' turn to offer their incense.

"The spirit of Mr. so and so," "The spirit of so and so"—the names of the deceased were read out loudly one by one, as the bonfire crackled. All of a sudden, I felt a chill running through my entire body, thinking of those lives taken by the earthquake in the early morning even before the sun was out. Then I thought to myself, "Perhaps people find this memorial event meaningful when they remember that day at the same time, at the same place and experience for themselves what people in the past have gone through in order to commemorate the lost lives." Slightly off to the side of the bonfire cans, an elderly man was talking to a group of girls who looked to be 4th to 6th graders, saying, "It must be hard for you all to imagine that that earthquake happened here. This entire area was covered by fire."

After each name of the deceased was read, the monk

> turned to the participants and gave a talk. The talk went something like this: Did you ever wonder why we pray? It's because we have memories. If we hold no memories, there is no need for prayers. The memories you have will continue to exist as long as you live, and that is something that cannot be erased. And what is required of us who are left behind is to live our lives to the fullest while preserving our memories of the deceased. After this short sermon, the event was over.
>
> While everybody headed home, a journalist was interviewing the woman, whose story we had overheard about her neighbor's passing. She explained how it was one of her neighbors that she had lost, but not her family members. The journalist thanked her and terminated the interview. Did he want to hear specific stories about losing family members, I wondered.
>
> The woman walked away and left the park. The moon hid itself behind the building and was no longer in our sight.

A memorial event like this takes place every year throughout the Kansai region (western Japan) on the day of the earthquake. You may have seen those events on TV or have even attended one because you have experienced some kind of natural disaster yourself. This account depicts the people who participated in a memorial ceremony, while illustrating the differences in how they take part in it. A middle-aged woman who was shouting the names of the deceased; a couple with a photograph of a young woman distancing themselves from the rest of the crowd; an elderly man who was talking to the younger elementary girls who had never experienced the earthquake; journalists who were interviewing the participants; monks who were in charge of the event. Everyone had his or her own story to tell, with specific intentions and their unique perspectives. We conducted a series of interviews with some of these people in order to learn more about their stories.

3. The Interviews
3.1 Participants

The participants of this study include Mr. Fujita, a *Soto* monk in his 40s who started this memorial event, Mr. Yamada in his 70s, a founder of a non-profit organization that supported the earthquake victims and has been assisting with the memorial event, Mr. Terada, in his 70s, who lost his daughter to the earthquake, and Mr. Ueki, in his 70s, who lost his mother to the earthquake, along with Mrs. Ueki, who is in her 60s. All participants, except for Mr. Terada, are fictitious names, as Mr. Terada, who was the one distancing himself from the crowd at the ceremony, strongly wished for his own name to be used for this study.

3.2 The History of the Service and the Participants' Meaning-Making

In this section, the narratives from the interviews reveal that all participants find this candle ceremony very meaningful in their own unique manner. In fact, we see many differences in how they understand their participation in the event. The following narrative reveals how it all started for Mr. Fujita.

> **Narrative 1:** *It was all personal in the beginning but ended up involving others.*
>
> Fujita: *Really, (apart from the official memorial service that took place a year after the earthquake,) it was just me asking other people if they would like to do it together. Ah, just volunteers. There was a kid's desk from a school with a flower vase and incense burner on it, right next to the prefab housing. It looked almost like an altar, but not really. But we decided to do it there anyway... and that's how the event came to be...*
>
> Kawashima (interviewer): *So, I understand that using candles is something that has changed since it became official (from the 7th anniversary). Has the ceremony procedure also changed?*
>
> Fujita: *No, as far as the memorial service is concerned, it hasn't changed. Well, yes, we've added structure to the event a bit since the number of participants increased. We read the Buddhist scripture and have everybody burn their incense as we do it today. That's all. Once that's done, then we preach a bit. It's as simple as that. Nearly nothing has changed since the very beginning.*

In the next two narratives, it becomes clear that this memorial service has a fair amount of influences on how the bereaved family has dealt with their grief processes. For example, in Narrative 2 by Mr. Ueki, he mentions that he felt the presence of Buddha by listening to the monk read the name of the deceased. In Narrative 3, Mr. Terada talks about how he feels like his heart is being cleansed and also feels encouraged with the sermon.

> **Narrative 2:** *The Buddhist Candle Memorial Service is a noble activity.*
>
> Ueki: *The candle lights flicker. Then I feel my mom's presence. Her name gets called. I put my hands together. Then, the face of Auntie Hayashi, Ishida, and various others appear. When the names that I don't know get called, I just say, "Namu Amida Butsu (Praise to Amida Buddha), Namu Amida Butsu." It's hard to describe, but while the monk calls out people's names—I feel that Buddha is very close. That the Buddha is present with us. That's why I think this candle service is a very noble activity.*
>
> **Narrative 3:** *The sermon cleanses my heart.*
>
> Terada: *The Soto monks often come for the memorial service as volunteers. When they come, what is it called, a sermon? At the end, they give a sermon, which really cleanses my heart and encourages me.*

3.3 The Buddhist Candle Memorial Service is Just as Important, but for Different Reasons

In this section, we will take a look at the content of each individual's unique interpretation as to why he or she has been involved with this event. Mr. Fujita, for example, mentions that it was his profound personal grief that drove him to start the memorial service, although he certainly recognized his role and expertise as a monk.

> **Narrative 4:** *I became involved out of my personal feelings.*
>
> Fujita: *The reasoning for the event, the Scriptures, the Canon and the sermon —all things religious and their surrounding concepts—all of them are after the fact. In the back of my mind, I*

had always felt that taking action for society itself is a religious matter. And I never felt I had to force myself to do so just because I am a monk, but rather, I did it out of my personal religious conscience, or my strong feeling [towards what happened during the earthquake].

Mr. Terada, in the meantime, clearly explains why he was distancing himself from the rest of the crowd during the service as described in the earlier field notes. He has been devoting this day to remembering his daughter every year at this place, and wishes to do so only for her sake.

Narrative 5: *On this day, I want to devote my prayer just for my daughter.*

Terada: *Since my daughter's passing on that day, I promised myself that I would go to the place where she passed and offer up my prayer for her at 5:46 a.m. ...Some journalists ask why I don't participate in front of the memorial monument with everyone else. But for me, January 17th is my daughter's memorial day. I want to devote my prayer to my daughter only. After doing that, I make sure to go towards the monument and pray for many others whose lives were lost.*

Mr. Terada is also critical of the entertainment part of the memorial service which sometimes takes place after the service. His comment in the following excerpt highlights different expectations regarding the memorial service among those who lost their loved ones and those participants who emphasize the restoration of the city.

Narrative 6: *Entertainment does nothing to heal my heart.*

Terada: *It's hard to describe, but many of those who participate in this event did not lose their family members. The pain that we as a bereaved family experienced is quite different from those who just lost their houses. Last time, a taiko (traditional Japanese drum) group came in after the service and performed. But honestly, it did nothing to heal my heart. Whenever there is an entertainment like that, I just go home, especially after all the monks have left the site.*

Mr. Yamada, who is a chair of an NPO for earthquake relief, on the other hand, finds the memorial event, including the entertainment, meaningful due to the fact that it brings back those who have left the area and reconnects them. As Miki (2001) states, the word "religion" originates from *re-ligare* in Latin, which means to "reconnect." It is clear that both Mr. Terada and Mr. Yamada position this memorial service as a ritual that "reconnects" Mr. Terada to his daughter and Mr. Yamada for the entire community."

Narrative 7: *Being connected, bringing people back together.*

Yamada: *I would like to say that people in our community are connected, instead of just living. And that feeling of connectedness comes about through opportunities such as our memorial service. ...The purpose [of the memorial service] is certainly to bring those who drifted apart back together, showing that people in this district are still lively and well.*

Mr. Ueki, who lost his mother, on the other hand, claims that one of the reasons why he participates in this Memorial Service is that he wants to express his appreciation to Mr. Yamada who has been helping with community restoration painstakingly for many years (narrative 8).

Narrative 8: *I want to show my appreciation to Mr. Yamada.*

Ueki: *The thing is, I want to please Mr. Yamada. Truly. He is making so many sacrifices in order to make this event happen. I think she [his deceased mother] would definitely approve that we help to support someone like Mr. Yamada. Someone who works so hard despite all the criticism from those around. ...So yes, it's out of gratitude that I participate in the Buddhist Candle Memorial Service.*

Further, as described in the following excerpt, people have different opinions about this memorial event itself. Mr. Ueki's wife does not attend the memorial service at all because she feels as though her mother-in-law is at the Buddhist altar at home. As a result, Mrs. Ueki always stays at home on this day to be with her. This illustrates how people, even within the same family, have different interpretations of the same tragedy.

Narrative 9: *I don't want to go anywhere else.*

(Mrs.) Ueki: *It's strange, but for me, I decided that I would be here [in front of the Buddhist altar at home] on the morning of January 17th. I just don't feel like going anywhere else. Yeah, I have this feeling that I don't want to go.*

Takeda (interviewer): *Do you have any particular reason why?*

(Mrs.) Ueki: *You know, I just feel like, being alone. So, when that time comes, I cannot but think about the way she died, you know.*

Takeda: *That's why you feel as though your mother-in-law is at the Buddhist altar.*

(Mrs.) Ueki: *Yes, yes, yes. I don't know why... it's strange. That's why I can't leave her alone here. That's why.*

In the preceding section, we described how various narratives depict "what we no longer have" and "religion as a way to live for the future" despite such a loss. Previous studies have found significant relationships between religious beliefs and practices and the psychological adjustment in the aftermath of disasters. Specifically, in times of distress, these findings reveal that positive religious coping strengthens interpersonal relationships while reducing the stress level (Meisenhelder, 2013), and that negative religious coping is related to depression and traumas (e.g., Feder et al., 2013). What was not revealed in those previous studies is the complexity that surrounds the process of grieving as well as the role of religion. To this end, this study, comprised of a series of in-depth interviews, revealed that the meanings people find in religion in times of distress are flexible, dynamic, and they depend on various contextual factors such as the passage of time, to whom they are told, and how they narrate their own stories.

4. Conclusion

This study reveals that people find a religious event like the Buddhist Candle Memorial Service meaningful in various ways. The meaning-making processes people find in religion are unique to each and every one of them, as they are comprised of multiple layers of narratives, which may or may not overlap with that of others. Drawing a simple causal relationship between religion and psychological adjustment after a loved one's loss does not necessarily help us understand how and why people find religion meaningful, nor does an assumption that religious leaders are the source and the bereaved family members are the recipients of religious messages. The qualitative method (Kawashima, 2011) we employed in this study enables us to see the complexities embedded in a specific context.

To conclude this chapter, let's take a look at Mr. Terada's statement.

Terada: *The truth is, what happened in Kobe is lost in time. People are getting tired of hearing about it. It won't be received well if we bring it up, which makes it difficult for us to talk about it... Surely people in Kobe have already forgotten about it except for those who have been affected by it. I wonder what they see when all 6,430 candles light up. They probably don't see anything. Even though they were born and raised in Kobe and have experienced the earthquake, they don't see it. The candles are there, trying their best to remind us all about what happened. That's how I see it.*

The candles are there so that people won't forget. As all the interviewees in this study similarly mentioned, the Buddhist Candle Memorial Service is thought of as a great reminder of many lives that have been lost, of the pain and struggles people left behind experienced, as well as of the fact that people have lived their lives despite tragedy. Undoubtedly, religion was a part of what held them together to help them continue on with their lives. Perhaps religion has played an essential role in remembering the lost lives, survivors, severely damaged town, and the disaster itself. The earthquake took many peoples' lives and forced the survivors to find meaning in their lives in order to live on. Although we cannot know how those who do not participate in the service see it, and the way it is understood varies from person to person, the roles religion plays in people's meaning-making processes are too great to be overlooked. "Do not forget"— that's the most important lesson we learned from this study. It is our hope that this study, too, helps us all to remember the lost lives and the struggles people have gone through, as well as the future they all strive to live for.

3.

People Living in Faith Traditions: Understanding the Meaning of "Faith" in Japan

Shuki Aizawa, Atomi University

1. What is "Faith"?
1.1 Modern Protestantism and the Concept of "Faith"

What would your answer be for the following questions: "Do you have a religion?" "Do you have faith?" Most people will answer either as "yes" or "no" to these questions. How, then, would you answer to the question, "Describe what religion or faith means to you." It's easy to see that having a religion or faith is one thing, but being able to explain the doctrine or one's own philosophy about them is another. In most cases, people would barely manage to explain their loosely held images of religion or faith, if anything at all. One may have a certain image or standard when it comes to making decisions as to what religion or faith is, but explaining it is quite difficult.

Defining religion or faith has always been a central issue in the studies of religion. Some critics even say that there are as many definitions as the number of researchers. Whether discussing the essence of religion or developing a working hypothesis for research analysis, "religion" had often been thought of as a matter of an individual's consciousness in the form of "faith." Recent studies, however, challenge such a simplistic view of religion originally promulgated by Modern Protestantism (e.g., Isomae, 2003; Tsuruoka, 2004). Instead, many researchers now suggest that faith means not only the conscious thoughts and feelings about obeying and trusting a supernatural being, but also the unconscious behavior and intuitions associated with one's experience, language, and senses as a whole.

1.2 Quantitative Approach to Faith in Japan

In an attempt to reveal Japanese people's religiosity, various research teams and newspapers have conducted quantitative surveys, which include questions such as the ones mentioned at the beginning of this chapter. According to those surveys, the number of those who have any kind of faith has decreased since the end of WWII, and less than only 30% of Japanese have some form of faith today (Ishii, 2007).

The question lies in the ambiguity of the word "faith." Quantitative researches rarely define the word, or explain the theoretical framework of their research. Consequently, participants are left to interpret survey questions on their own, leaving all of us wondering what "the declining number of those who have faith" actually means.

1.3 The Obstacles in Quantitative Approach

Due to the multifaceted character of faith as a psychological construct, there are many obstacles to capturing the images of religion or faith that people have when using a quantitative approach. Whether researchers and participants share the same understanding of these images is one of these obstacles. In order to overcome some of those difficulties, researchers have tried asking people about the contents and intensity of their faith as well as about their motivation, and yet the limitations, which come with quantitative methodology, have posed a tremendous barrier to capturing what "religion" and "faith" truly mean to Japanese people. While a qualitative approach such as fieldwork and in-depth interviews is better for this particular quest, it also comes with shortcomings. Requiring much less time and lighter workloads, a quantitative approach then allows us to efficiently collect data in bulk, objectively turning them into meaningful numbers, and quantifying the relationships among variables.

The J-MARS study described here investigated Japanese religiosity from a more holistic viewpoint than conventional "yes" or "no" questions about faith. Besides the basic demographics such as gender and age, we asked participants to identify one of five religious categories that they ascribe themselves to: "Buddhism," "*Shintoism*," "Christianity," "Others," and "Do not have faith."[1] In order to achieve our goal of capturing the diversity and multi-dimensionality of the Japanese religiosity, we conducted various statistical analyses on the acquired data (see Appendix for more details).

2. Results
2.1 People with Faith

40.1% of our sample (n = 2,475) responded that they have faith in one of the religions ("Buddhism," "*Shintoism*," "Christianity," or "Others") as compared to 59.9% who did not ("Do not have faith") (n = 3,696). (The total is n = 6,171 that excludes missing data[2]). Among those with faith, 57.1% identified with "Christianity," while 37.6% chose "Buddhism" as a basis of their faith. Much less than 10% chose "*Shintoism*" and "Others" (Figure 3.1). Here, it is important to note that claiming to have faith in a certain religion does not necessarily mean he or she has a membership in those religious institutions. It simply means that that is the religion he or she is most interested in. For example, one may not belong to any religious group yet may identify Buddhism as a basis of their faith. Thus, in this chapter we decided to conceptualize those religious groups as "Interested Religious Groups."

This result contradicts Ishii's (2007) findings in which the majority of the people chose Buddhism as Interested Religious Groups and very few did so for Christianity. This could be due to sample biases, as our study included many people who have close ties with Christianity. Despite getting samples from various types of institutions (e.g., community centers, public schools, religious schools) as well as from five different religious groups, Christianity-related people made up the majority in our study. The sample also included religious leaders (e.g., Christian priests, pastors, and Buddhist monks). In order to keep these religious leaders separate from others who are merely interested in specific religious groups, we labeled those general participants as "affiliates."

2.2 The Image of Religion and Faith

Christianity and Buddhism are often the subject of comparison when it comes to religious faith in Japan. For Christianity, frequent churchgoers who believe in Jesus of Nazareth as the Christ (the Messiah) are a common image of Christianity in Japan. In the case of Buddhism, people usually associate it with widely practiced religious customs such as memorial services for ancestors or the deceased, rather than "devoting one's life to the Buddhist doctrine." The Buddhist parishioner (*danka*) system, a relationship between a family and a temple that is sustained over many generations, has a long history in Japan, and has likely influenced how Japanese people think of Buddhism. In this survey, we did not ask how well they understood religious doctrine or about the frequency of their visits to religious facilities. However, the result showed a distinct difference as to how those religious affiliates conceptualized their own faith.

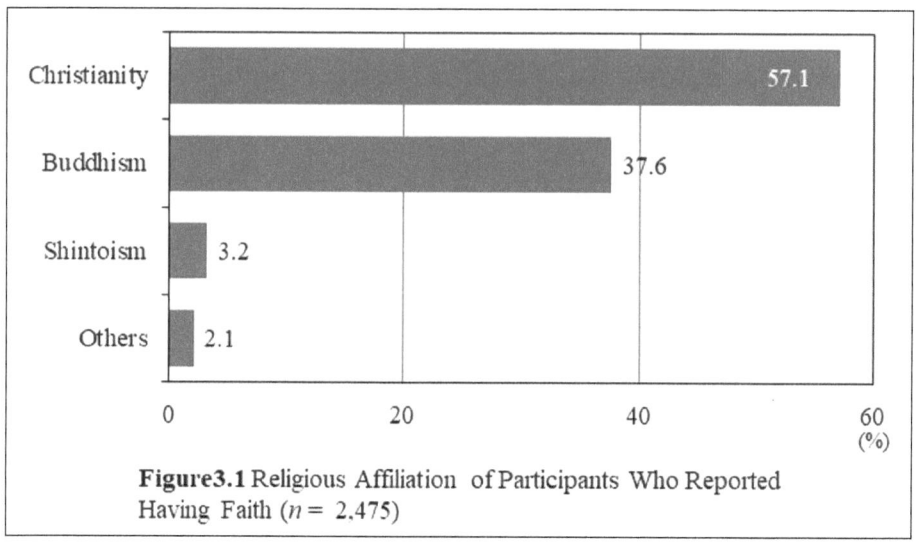

Figure 3.1 Religious Affiliation of Participants Who Reported Having Faith ($n = 2,475$)

Among Christian affiliates, 94.3% of Catholic ($n = 66$) and 98.3% of Protestant Christians ($n = 740$) responded that they have faith in Christianity. Interestingly, 2.9% Catholic ($n = 2$) and 1.7% Protestant Christians ($n = 13$) responded that they do not have faith, and 2.9% of Catholics ($n = 2$) even identified Buddhism as the basis of their faith. Among Buddhist (*Soto* Zen Buddhism) affiliates, 65.4% ($n = 100$) chose Buddhism as a basis of their faith, and as many as 33.3% ($n = 51$) responded that they did not have a faith. More surprisingly, nearly 20% responded either that the temple they belonged to was not a part of their denomination (11.8%), or that they did not know whether their temple was a part of *Soto* Zen Buddhism (7.7%). However, affiliates of the *Rissho-kosei-kai*, a Buddhist denomination included in this study, had a result similar to the Christian groups, in that only 0.4% ($n = 1$) responded that they did not have faith, while 93.8% ($n = 225$) chose Buddhism as a basis of their faith.

2.3 Discussion: Capturing Faith without Presumptions

When we regard someone as "Christian" or "Buddhist," it is almost automatically assumed that he or she believes in those respective doctrines. Religious doctrines are the records of the teachings of the founders, giving believers guidance that transcends geographical, societal, and generational differences. The absence of those original religious founders leaves rooms for interpretations, bringing life to its teachings to be passed on from one generation to another. The current study does not reveal to what extent those believers actually read the original sources of the teachings, but for Buddhism affiliates, many of them most likely rely on priests or monks to gain a better understanding.

In fact, in *Soto* Zen Buddhism, one of the largest Buddhism sects in Japan, the affiliates seem to pay little attention to its doctrine and teachings. For example, the results of our study as well as other surveys by the *Soto*-Buddhism organizations found that most of the affiliates are extremely indifferent regarding its primary "religious doctrine," (namely, the practice of *zazen* or sitting meditation and strictly adhering to the Buddhist Precepts, striving to be awakened by realizing that one's soul is the Buddha") and "religious teaching" (that is "following the primary principles in *shushougi*, the practice of the truth that striving/training itself is enlightenment") (Survey Committee, 2014). However, it would be a mistake to say that they do not believe in the doctrine based solely on these results. Rather, *Soto* Zen Buddhism affiliates are "led by" listening to monks preaching at memorial services for ancestors. Their preaching may not be directly related to the doctrine itself, yet the affiliates who listen to it receive it as a teaching of Buddha and accept it as guidance to live a better life.

Although having faith and believing in religious doctrine are often considered the same, I believe that these two things are not necessarily the same. In order to gain a holistic view of Japanese religiosity, religious sentiment and unspoken, unconscious elements of their religious attitude ought not be ignored. Buddhism affiliates gain such religiously rich experience through the preaching that they hear at religious ceremonies and rituals. The widely-accepted assumptions regarding faith often misguide researchers; we will discuss this matter further later in the chapter.

3. Growth and Faith
3.1 Demographics and Faith

People come to believe in religion for various reasons. Using relative deprivation theory, a famous sociologist C. Glock constructed typologies and explained the types of religion that certain people are attracted to. In the fields of both the sociology and psychology of religion, the reason people with anxiety, life troubles and various difficulties are often drawn to religion has been a subject of studies for a long time. Cults and their surrounding social issues also have been a major focus for the sociology of religion, and countless studies have investigated why a certain religion attracts certain people. The purpose of this study is the same as previous studies, but with a different perspective. We investigated the characteristics of Japanese people with faith, including priests and monks, in order to better understand their religiosity.

37.7% of men and 41.3% of women responded that they have faith. The total number of male and female participants was 2,159 and 4,000 respectively. 62.3% men and 58.7% women responded that they do not have faith, which is approximately 20% more than those who have faith for both genders. According to a *chi* square analysis and a subsequent analysis on the adjusted residuals, men are less likely to have faith than not to have faith, whereas the opposite is true for women (See table 3.1)[3]. This result is consistent with previous findings.

Table 3.1 Gender and Faith

Gender [n (%)]	Faith		Total
	Have faith	Do not have faith	
Men	813 (37.7)	1,346 (62.3)	2,159 (100.0)
Adjusted residual	-2.8**	2.8**	
Women	1,652 (41.3)	2,348 (58.7)	4,000 (100.0)
Adjusted residual	2.8**	-2.8**	
Total	2,465 (40.0)	3,694 (60.0)	6,159 (100.0)
$\chi^2(1, n = 6,159) = 7.76$, **$p < .01$			

The participant's average age for those with faith was 41.0 years (Mdn = 42.0) and for those without was 18.5 years (Mdn = 17.0). The total number of participants included in this analysis was 6,113. Looking at the relationship between age and faith more closely, it was found that the average age difference between those with faith and without faith was statistically significant (See table 3.2)[4]. This result suggests that people are likely to gain faith sometime between these two ages.

Table 3.2 Age and Faith

	n	Mean age	SD	t-value	df
People with faith	2,450	41.04	23.85	45.18**	2,820.26
People without faith	3,663	18.47	7.99		

**p < .01

3.2 Life Experience and Faith

Previous studies have found that the older one gets, the more likely it is that he or she has faith. The age increase generally means more life experience. Work, marriage, giving birth, raising children, and deaths of loved ones all help one grow and mature as a person. We conducted a chi-square test in order to see if our results support this hypothesis. Table 3.3 shows that among adolescents (12~25 years old, equivalent to middle, high school and college students), there are more people without faith than those with faith. On the other hand, among working adults (26~64 years old), there are more people with faith than those without. This was also the case for the non-working adults, of which 64.3% (n = 637) are older adults (65~93 years old).

Although it cannot be proven, the results seem to suggest that the depth of life experience is correlated with the emergence of faith. As shown in Table 3.4 and 3.5, there are more people with faith among those who are married, have children, and so forth. Having experienced the struggles as well as the joys of life seems to influence whether or not people have faith.

Table 3.3 Work and Faith

Work [n (%)]	Faith		Total
	Have faith	Do not have faith	
Junior high school students	406 (27.8)	1,055 (72.2)	1,461 (100.0)
Adjusted residual	-10.1**	10.1**	
High school students	301 (19.3)	1,257 (80.7)	1,558 (100.0)
Adjusted residual	-18.5**	18.5**	
College students	348 (23.0)	1,165 (77.0)	1,513 (100.0)
Adjusted residual	-14.8*	14.8*	
Working adults (Full-time)	484 (79.0)	129 (21.0)	613 (100.0)
Adjusted residual	21.4**	-21.4**	
Working adults (Part-time)	232 (86.2)	37 (13.8)	269 (100.0)
Adjusted residual	16.2**	-16.2**	
Non-working adults	588 (93.0)	44 (7.0)	632 (100.0)
Adjusted residual	29.4**	-29.4**	
Total	2,359 (39.0)	3,687 (61.0)	6,046 (100.0)

$\chi^2(5, n = 6{,}046) = 1{,}932.83$, **p < .01

Table 3.4 Marital Status and Faith

Marital status [n (%)]	Faith		Total
	Have faith	Do not have faith	
Married	1,180 (88.7)	150 (11.3)	1,330 (100.0)
Adjusted residual	31.9**	-31.9**	
Never married	560 (31.4)	1,223 (68.6)	1,783 (100.0)
Adjusted residual	-31.9**	31.9**	
Total	1,740 (55.9)	1,373 (44.1)	3,113 (100.0)

$\chi^2(1, n = 3,113) = 1,015.04$, **$p < .01$

Table 3.5 Whether Having Child(ren) (or not) and Faith

Children [n (%)]	Faith		Total
	Have faith	Do not have faith	
Have	1,107 (89.9)	125 (10.1)	1,232 (100.0)
Adjusted residual	30.7**	-30.7**	
Do not have	643 (34.0)	1,247 (66.0)	1,890 (100.0)
Adjusted residual	-30.7**	30.7**	
Total	1,750 (56.1)	1,372 (43.9)	3,122 (100.0)

$\chi^2(1, n = 3,122) = 943.82$, **$p < .01$

3.3 Loss and Faith

Some researchers say that religion exists because of death. Death certainly is a distinctive event in our lives, and world religions have encouraged us to leave such matter to the eternal, immutable dictates of god(s) or the universe. However, as those religions become widely accepted and practiced worldwide, various rituals and teachings regarding death have evolved. Japan is no exception: most Japanese bid farewell to the dead with Buddhism-style funeral, and visit their graves regularly.

Since most Japanese people participate in these Buddhism rituals as they grow up, one may expect that those experiences have had certain impact on whether they have faith or not. In our survey, we asked participants if they have a family grave in which to bury their own ashes, and if they have attended someone's funeral before.

Table 3.6 shows the results of a chi square analysis and a subsequent analysis of adjusted residuals. It was found that those who have a family grave are more likely to have faith than not to have faith, while those who do not have a family grave are more likely to have no faith. Similarly, we also tested if there is any relationship between funeral experiences and having faith (Table 3.7). It was found that those who have experienced funerals in the past are likely to have faith than not to have faith. The opposite was true for those who have never attended a funeral.

Table 3.6 Family Grave and Faith

Family grave [n (%)]	Faith		Total
	Have faith	Do not have faith	
Have	1,899 (45.6)	2,270 (54.4)	4,169 (100.0)
Adjusted residual	11.7**	-11.7**	
Do not have	529 (29.4)	1,273 (70.6)	1,802 (100.0)
Adjusted residual	-11.7**	11.7**	
Total	2,428 (40.7)	3,543 (59.3)	5,971 (100.0)

$\chi^2(1, n = 5,971) = 136.75$, **$p < .01$

Table 3.7 Funeral Experiences and Faith

Funeral experiences [n (%)]	Faith		Total
	Have faith	Do not have faith	
Have	2,022 (43.2)	2,659 (56.8)	4,681 (100.0)
Adjusted residual	8.2**	-8.2**	
Do not have	431 (30.9)	964 (69.1)	1,395 (100.0)
Adjusted residual	-8.2**	8.2**	
Total	2,453 (40.4)	3,623 (59.6)	6,076 (100.0)

$\chi^2(1, n = 6,076) = 67.54$, **$p < .01$

3.4 Succession of Faith

The result so far has shown that gender, age, marital status, and various life events all have impact on whether or not one has faith. Since most Japanese participate in Buddhist practices growing up, their religious experience is quite passive. Take an example of a typical Japanese individual who grows up going to a family temple with his or her parents. The person has never taken an interest in Buddhism per se, and does not know anything about a particular sect. When a parent dies, he or she finally learns the name of the sect his family temple belongs to, and becomes involved with Buddhism (Aizawa, 2016). For this person, it was out of necessity as well as family custom that he or she contacted the temple in order to hold a funeral. Likewise, the person did not have choice as a child whether or not he or she goes to the temple because it was decided by the parents. In such cases, which are very common in Japan, we can assume that family religion greatly influences one's faith.

In the survey, we asked participants if they inherited their faith from their parents. The result showed that among those who have faith ($n = 2,330$), 57.0% inherited while 43.0% responded that they did not inherit the faith. For the latter group, it may have been their grandparents or friends who influenced their faith, or a personal choice that they made on their own. Either way, more than half of the population's faith was inherited from their parents.

Next, we conducted a chi-square analysis to see the relationship between religious groups and inheritance (Table 3.8). The result showed that there are more people with inherited faith than those without in Buddhism, while the opposite was true for Christians. There was no difference for *Shinto* and other religious group categories. In summary, those who chose Buddhism as a basis of their faith are more likely to inherit faith from their parents in comparison with other religions.

Table 3.8 Religious Groups and Inheritance of Faith

Religious groups [n (%)]	Inheritance of faith from parents		Total
	Yes	No	
Buddhism	767 (85.7)	128 (14.3)	895 (100.0)
Adjusted residual	22.1**	-22.1**	
Shintoism	43 (56.6)	33 (43.4)	76 (100.0)
Adjusted residual	-0.1	0.1	
Christianity	491 (37.5)	819 (62.5)	1,310 (100.0)
Adjusted residual	-21.5**	21.5**	
Others	26 (53.1)	23 (46.9)	49 (100.0)
Adjusted residual	-0.6	0.6	
Total	1,327 (57.0)	1,003 (43.0)	2,330 (100.0)

$\chi^2(3, n = 2,330) = 504.55$, **$p < .01$

4. Who and How: Characteristics of People with Faith in Japan
4.1 Understanding Religiosity: Pros and Cons of Psychometric Scales

The results so far revealed the demographics of Japanese people with faith and the relationship among the variables. But the question of Japanese religiosity still remains unanswered. As previously noted, the psychology of religion developed in Western countries around the 19th century, and it has been structured around Christianity. Simply put, religiosity has been narrowly defined as an individual's consciousness towards what is beyond this world's order. Further, in an attempt to expand the scope of its inquiry, many psychometric scales based on Christian assumptions have been created and tested. Especially understanding religiosity as unconscious actions, attitudes or senses rather than consciousness has received much attention in recent years.

A psychometric scale allows researchers to measure and quantify religiosity. Participants generally respond to a *Likert*-Scale, such as "Strongly disagree," "Disagree," "Neither," "Agree," "Strongly agree." The data are then analyzed using techniques such as factor analysis by grouping items that are closely related. Through examination of each item within a group, a researcher then will name each factor and create a typology. There are two major issues that might produce a biased outcome in this process: creating survey questions and naming factors.

Whether consciously or unconsciously, a researcher's underlying thoughts and premises about his or her own religious convictions, which often are based on Protestant Christianity, influence the research questions and the labeling of the factors. Naturally, these processes produce results that are consistent with the presumed Christian values and ideas. This is less problematic if a researcher is aware of his or her assumptions. However, when a researcher is unaware of his or her own biases and overgeneralizes, the findings for all types of religiosity and the validity of the scale will be in question. Understanding religiosity as an attitude is a fairly new idea, and we must be well aware of these pitfalls when analyzing the results.

4.2 Religious Belief Scale

The Religious Belief Scale (Kaneko, 1997) is a commonly used religiosity scale in Japan with three factors: 1) Pro-religiousness, 2) Belief in Guardianship, and 3) Belief in the Soul. The questions include:

1) Pro-religiousness
   Having a religious life gives a purpose to life

   A life imbued with a religious faith is a person's true way of living

   Religious faith is necessary in order to lead a good life

   Religion does not reveal the meaning of life

   No matter how advanced science becomes, humankind could never be happy without a faith

2) Belief in Guardianship
   I feel close to Kannon and Fudo-myoo

   I feel hesitant to participate in old customs and annual religious events

Ancestor worship is a beautiful custom

Being in the premises of a Shinto shrine brings peace of mind at times

I feel an affinity towards religious events such as Bon Festival

3) Belief in the Soul
I believe that there is life after death

If you believe in Buddha or the gods and pray for the fulfillment of your wishes, your prayers will be realized eventually

Human beings will be born again after death

I think that a deceased person's spirit will curse us if we do not hold a memorial service for the repose of his or her soul

There will be consequences if a person disrespects Buddha and the gods

Table 3.9 The Means (SD) of Scores of Religious Belief Scale Among the Religious Groups, and Result of One-Way ANOVA

Subscales	Buddhists	Shintoists	Christians	Others	No faith	F (df)
Pro-religiousness	19.87 (5.66)	18.27 (5.56)	23.77 (5.14)	19.79 (6.20)	14.71 (4.03)	1,014.49**
	909	78	1,343	52	3,620	(4, 5,997)
Belief in Guardianship	22.58 (3.87)	24.36 (3.67)	16.09 (5.05)	21.44 (5.38)	19.01 (4.03)	351.04**
	914	77	1,339	50	3,603	(4, 5,978)
Belief in Soul	19.76 (4.16)	21.01 (4.39)	16.42 (4.49)	18.88 (5.04)	18.28 (4.72)	82.08**
	880	76	1,313	52	3,608	(4, 5,924)

Subscales	Result of the multiple comparisons analysis [Tukey's method]
Pro-religiousness	Christians > Buddhists = Shintoists = Others > No faith**
Belief in Guardianship	Shintoists > Buddhists = Others > No faith > Christians**
Belief in Soul	Buddhists = Shintoists > No faith > Christians**, Others > Christians**

**$p < .01$

In our project, we analyzed the data using one-way ANOVA as well as multiple comparisons in order to see if there is any difference among the religious groups (Table 3.9). The total score of religious groups for each factor is displayed below from the highest group to the lowest.

1) Inclination towards Religions:
   Christians> Buddhists=Shintoists=Others>No faith

2) Sense of Protection from Ancestors:
   Shintoists>Buddhists=Others>No faith>Christians

3) Belief in an Immortal Soul:
   Buddhists=Shintoists>No faith=Others>Christianity

For "Inclination towards Religions," Christians scored the highest, presumably due to the items that focus on the highly conscious aspect of faith. Although Buddhism, too, assumes individual faith just like Christianity, the cultural, societal, and historical context in Japan did not always allow individuals to make conscious decisions regarding faith. As explained earlier, Buddhism has been tied to the family through the Buddhist-parishioner system since the Edo period, and this practice has been fortified through cultural traditions such as annual memorial services for the dead for generations. That is, for many individuals, their inclination towards Buddhism is an unconscious choice facilitated by these traditions. Thus, the history behind the spread of Buddhist practice seems to explain the significant gap between Christianity and Buddhism on Inclination towards Religions.

"The Sense of Receiving Protection from Ancestors" consists of items that evoke Japanese customs and common practices, which explains why *Shintoists* scored the highest, followed by a home-grown Buddhists and Others, which both scored significantly higher than "No faith," while Christians scored the lowest. It was understandably so since none of those items are necessarily compatible with Christian teaching that opposes idolatry. Incompatibility between Christian teachings and local customs such as this has always been a critical issue for Christian missionaries, and Japan was no exception. When Jesuit Francis Xavier came to Japan to spread Christianity around 16th century, widely practiced Buddhism memorial services for the dead and ancestors imposed some serious challenges. To determine whether or not Japanese Christians could attend Buddhism-style funerals and memorial services, the

Jesuit missionaries sought a judgment from the Roman theologians who concluded that those practices are nothing more than an act of honoring the dead, not an act of worshiping them, and thus these are non-religious customs. Therefore, Japanese Christians were allowed to attend Buddhism style funerals so long as they did not desecrate the Christian God.

Modern Christianity in Japan still faces the same issue. The Second Vatican Council (1962~1965) opted for a policy to respect other religious traditions as well as different cultures, which encouraged the Japanese Catholic church to allow attendance at Buddhism style funerals or to keep *ihai* (memorial tablets or mementoes of the deceased) at home. Those customs, however, are still foreign to Catholic churches, and showing a special appreciation of or fascination with them is by no means encouraged. In fact, in our data, while the mid-point (neither "agree" nor "disagree") under this category is 17.5, Christians scored 16.09. Being torn between Christian teachings and Japanese customs perhaps skewed their average scores more towards "disagree" rather than the "agree."

"Belief in an Immortal Soul" includes items such as an afterlife, reincarnation, and retribution. Buddhists and *Shintoists* scored the highest, as these characteristics are all familiar to and accepted by many. However, Christians scored lower than those with "No faith," negatively responding to the items with the average score below the mid-point (16.42). This result again reflects the fact that while Christian teachings may accept the idea of the afterworld, other notions such as reincarnation and karma, do not match their worldview

4.3 Discussion

Looking at the three factors of Japanese religiosity closely, we noticed that they were generated from a dichotomous conceptualization of religiosity: doctrine and faith on one hand and folkways and rituals on the other. Although their contents may vary, "Inclination towards Religiosity" relates to doctrines while a "Sense of Protection from Ancestors" and "Belief in an Immortal Soul" relates to folkways. The result seems to suggest that the former element is emphasized among people identifying with Christianity, while the latter is emphasized among *Buddhists* and *Shintoists*. Interestingly, the participants seem to endorse such categorization, reflecting their dichotomous concept of religion.

For many religions, folkways have always been considered a deviation and thus a threat to a given doctrine. Examples in Buddhism include funeral rituals and the benefits gained in this world through observance of the Buddhist teachings. Another example in Christianity includes a belief in purgatory. All have been a target of criticism, since they deviate from the original doctrines and the teachings of the respective religions. Yet again, such arguments exist solely due to the influence of Modern Protestantism, which pursues doctrine-oriented faith. Though this is not a place to discuss the validity of those arguments, our study successfully shed light on some of those underlying premises that Protestant Christianity has taken up. To conclude, when looked at broadly and without bias, we cannot help but wonder if one may see an image of religion as well as a form of faith that previous studies have not yet discovered.

Notes:

[1] We also asked the participants who answered other than "Do not have faith" to specify which denomination they belong to. They include the *Jodoshinshu Soto* sect, etc. for "Buddhism," *Izumo-taisha-kyo*, *Tenri-kyo*, etc. for "Shintoism," Catholic, Holiness Church, etc. for "Christianity," and Church of PL, Soka Gakkai, etc. for "Others."

[2] Missing data include those with missing data and/or invalid responses.

[3] Table 3.1 depicts the number of people who either "Have faith" or "Do not have faith," and whether the difference between the two is statistically significant from each other. In this case, if the adjusted residuals are greater than +2.58, it means that the observed frequency is greater than the expected frequency. For example, 1,652 (observed frequency of women with faith) is greater than the expected frequency, indicating women is likely to have faith than not have faith, adjusted for sample size. In contrast, if the residuals are less than -2.58, it means that the observed frequency is less than the expected frequency. That is, 2,348 (observed frequency of women without faith) is less than the expected frequency, indicating women is less likely to not have faith than to have faith. The rest of the analysis on adjusted residuals in this chapter follows the same rule. Note also that the total number of the data in these tables may vary due to missing data.

[4] The result is based on a *t*-test with "having or not having religious faith" as an independent variable while chronological age as dependent variable.

4.

Japanese Religiosity through the Lens of Psychological Health: The Role of Religion in Seeking a Better Life

Masahiro Nakao, Osaka Ohtani University

1. Introduction

"What is psychological health?" Although hard to define, countless studies in various fields, including psychology, have dealt with this topic. As the World Health Organization's (WHO) definition of health includes physical, mental, and social facets, a recent debate has suggested that "spirituality" should be an integral part of this definition as well. According to this line of debate, then, spirituality and religiosity may also influence psychological health.

Further, since a majority of the studies on religiosity and the broadly construed concept of psychological health have been carried out in Western countries, similar investigations in non-Western, multi-religious contexts like Japan should be carried out as well. In this chapter, I will present findings from the J-MARS project that involves various populations such as middle school, high school, and university students, general working adults, and those who are active members of five different religious organizations (Catholic, Protestant, *Soto*-Buddhism, *Shintoism*, Rissho-kosei-kai Buddhism). It is my hope to shed light on the question of whether religion is necessary for us to be psychologically healthy as we all face life's inevitable pain and hardship.

2. Mental Health and Well-Being from a Perspective of Health Psychology

Health psychology is an applied behavioral field that focuses on the issues related to human health. It is assumed that both physiological and psychological health equally contribute to one's overall health. From this perspective, how should human health be defined? It is not a mere absence of disease. According to WHO (1948), health is defined as "A state of complete physical, mental, and social well-being, not merely the absence of disease or infirmity."

Based on this definition, Shimai (1997) posits that in order to achieve a state of psychological health, one needs to go beyond the state without diseases, located in the mid-point between sickness and wellness in Figure 4.1. In Shimai's bio-psycho-social model of sickness and health, the bottom part of the left diagram in Figure 4.1 depicts the state with obstacles due to diseases. One's health improves as it proceeds from a state of illness, pre-illness state, healthy state as a middle-point, and onto the state with health awareness while sustaining optimal lifestyle.

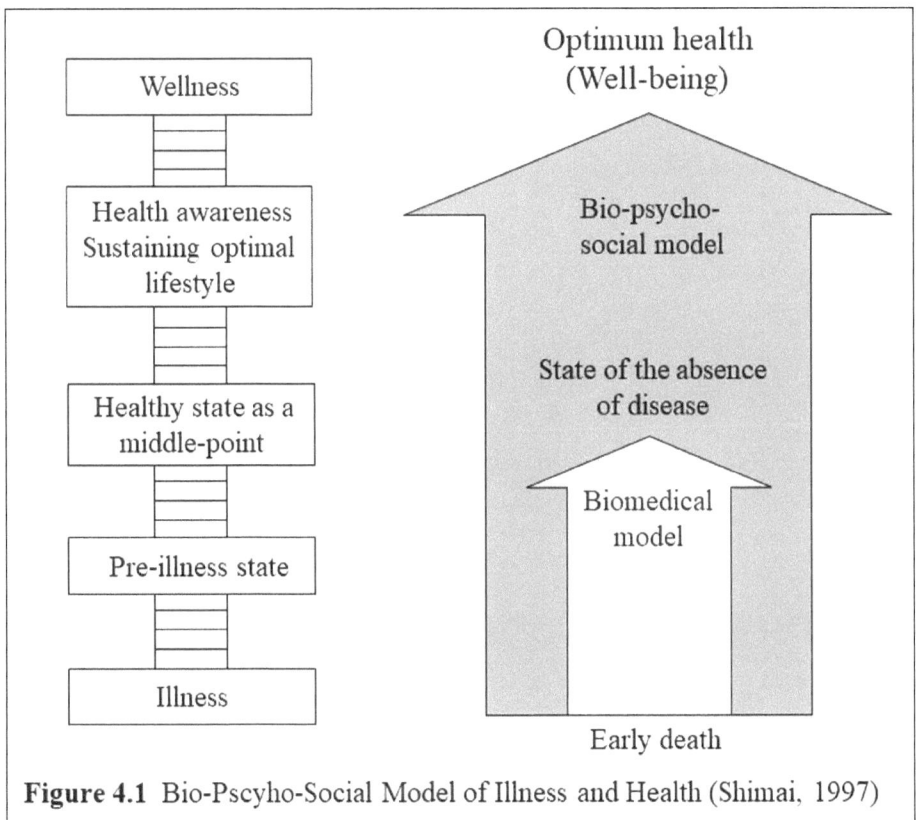

Figure 4.1 Bio-Pscyho-Social Model of Illness and Health (Shimai, 1997)

Ohishi (2006) suggests that one must understand what "being well" means in order to fully grasp a concept of "well-being." This type of inquiry opens up a philosophical question of what "well" means in well-being, "good" in a good person, and ultimately what constitutes an ideal person. For example, in the U.S., a "cheerful," "diplomatic," and "independent" person is generally considered ideal. Although these characteristics are regarded as favorable in Japan as well, many Japanese think of an ideal person as "someone who is accepted or approved of by others." In other words, the core of "well-being" is how close a person is to a given cultural image of an ideal person.

While many researchers continue to explore the meaning of "well-being," a lack of consensus on its definition remains problematic. However, researchers from different disciplines are also motivated to study this concept because of that. It is crucial, therefore, to continue studying "well-being" to fill the potential gap in its definition in different cultural contexts.

3. Data on Perception of Psychological Health Among Japanese

Sets of data were collected from various settings associated with five religious organizations: Catholic, Protestant, *Izumo-Taisha Shintoist*, *Soto* Buddhist, and *Rissho-kosei-kai* Buddhist. As shown in Figure 4.2, these groups can be located on the continuum of how frequently they have religion-related experiences.

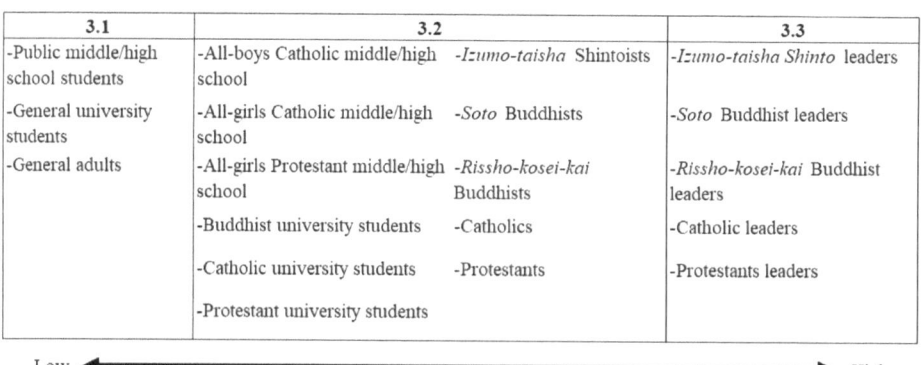

3.1	3.2		3.3
-Public middle/high school students	-All-boys Catholic middle/high school	-*Izumo-taisha* Shintoists	-*Izumo-taisha Shinto* leaders
-General university students	-All-girls Catholic middle/high school	-*Soto* Buddhists	-*Soto* Buddhist leaders
-General adults	-All-girls Protestant middle/high school	-*Rissho-kosei-kai* Buddhists	-*Rissho-kosei-kai* Buddhist leaders
	-Buddhist university students	-Catholics	-Catholic leaders
	-Catholic university students	-Protestants	-Protestants leaders
	-Protestant university students		

Low ⟵⟶ High
Frequency of having religion-related experiences

Figure 4.2 Frequency of Having Religion-Related Experiences in the Participants at Each Field Site

The survey included two questions. The first question was, "Do you know anyone who is psychologically healthy?" with "Yes" or "No" as a response. The second question was an open-ended question; "How do you describe a 'psychologically healthy person'? If you answered 'yes' in the first question, please describe that person. If you answered 'no,' please describe your own idea of such a person."

We analyzed the texts to identify the phrases describing a psychologically healthy person to extract keywords and then organized them based on how frequently they were mentioned. In this study, I report only the frequently used key words (see Table 4.1).

3.1 People with the Least Religion-Related Experiences (Public Middle/High School Students and General University Students and Adults)

Eighty-nine middle school students (47 boys, 39 girls, 3 N/A) and 397 high school students (211 boys, 180 girls, 6 N/A) participated in this survey. The average age for boys and girls was 14.9 (SD=0.3) and 16.8 (SD=1.0), respectively. Phrases related to the keywords empathy, thoughtfulness, and self-sacrifice appeared the most (91 words). Examples were "being empathetic to others" and "caring for others more than oneself." Phrases related to the keywords forward-thinking, positive-thinking, and cheerful appeared frequently as well (81 words). Examples included "willing to overcome difficulties" and "making hardships count for one's own growth." Other keywords included gentle and kind, followed by generous and self-assured. Examples related to these keywords included "willing to accept things for what they are" and "knowing oneself." In summary, for public middle and high school students, a psychologically healthy person is considered to be empathetic, thoughtful, cheerful, and kind. In other words, for teenagers, the characteristics related to interpersonal skills with and cheerful personality appeared to be related to psychological health.

General university students (who were recruited from non-religious universities) and adults (*N*=318) were grouped together (88 men, 224 women, 4 N/A). The average age was 31.4 (*SD*=13.8). Similar to the results with public middle/high school students, keywords like forward thinking and empathy appeared frequently, while feelings often associated with innocence and simplicity, such as kind or honesty, were emphasized as personalities of a psychologically healthy person. Example phrases were "turning negatives into positives," "speaking and acting considerately," and "being trustworthy at all times." A few included phrases related to religion such as "someone who has religious faith" and "someone who believes in God."

Table 4.1 Data on Perception of Psychological Health Among Each Groups

	Public middle/high school students	General adults/ university students	All-boys Catholic middle/high school	All-girls Catholic middle/high school	All-girls Protestant middle/high school	Religion-affiliated university students
Forward-thinking, positive-thinking, and cheerful	81	60	30	122	111	197
Empathy, thoughtfulness, and self-sacrifice	91	56	113	479	172	218
Honesty	33	45	44	128	77	132
Gentle and kind	57	44	96	168	208	97
Laughing a lot, fun-loving, and energetic	43	43	47	119	102	159
Others	*	22	*	41	*	*
Generous and fair	43	21	41	87	118	159
None/Uncertain	20	17	86	66	65	68
Not slandering	16	12	13	56	34	50
Self-assured	42	*	39	103	42	129
Religion-related	*	*	16	45	78	74
Not getting angry	*	*	*	*	*	20
Sensitive	*	*	*	*	*	18
Gratitude	*	*	*	*	*	*
Accepting	*	*	*	*	*	*
Hard-working and perseverance	*	*	*	*	*	*
Humility	*	*	*	*	*	*
Peaceful	*	*	*	*	*	*
Calm	*	*	*	*	*	*
Forgiving	*	*	*	*	8	*
Babies and children	*	*	*	*	*	*
Respectable	*	*	*	*	*	*
Impartiality	*	*	*	*	*	*
Good listener	*	*	*	*	*	*
Good interpersonal skills	*	*	*	*	*	*

These results suggest that there is little difference between public middle/high school students and general university students regarding the images of a psychologically healthy person. In other words, among people with the least religion-related experiences kind, gentle, empathetic, and cheerful are key to psychological health. However, it is interesting to note that this particular Japanese group emphasized the relationship with others (e.g., "caring for others more than oneself") more than the ones found in the West that focused more on individual characteristics and strengths (e.g., being "diplomatic and independent").

Furthermore, the keywords related to religion rarely appeared. This is possibly because, especially for the middle/high school students and university students, future planning and accomplishing daily tasks

atholics	Protestants	Soto Buddhists	Rissho-kosei-kai Buddhists	Izumo-taisha Shintoists	Catholic leaders	Protestants leaders	Soto Buddhist leaders	Rissho-kosei-kai Buddhist leaders
22	152	26	55	14	28	21	8	40
30	212	65	120	10	34	16	16	46
12	55	12	27	8	9	28	*	18
15	83	24	62	*	*	21	*	20
16	83	18	51	11	*	16	*	14
*	*	*	*	*	*	*	*	*
20	124	11	16	6	*	42	3	13
*	22	10	*	*	*	*	*	*
*	48	10	10	6	7	12	7	*
*	*	*	*	*	11	*	*	*
43	388	13	43	8	34	105	16	41
*	*	*	*	*	*	*	*	*
*	*	*	*	*	*	*	*	*
*	69	*	22	6	*	8	*	13
*	45	6	6	*	11	17	*	6
*	37	*	*	*	*	20	*	6
*	19	*	*	*	*	*	*	7
*	17	*	*	*	*	*	*	*
*	14	25	10	*	8	*	*	*
*	9	*	*	*	*	*	*	*
*	9	*	*	*	*	*	*	*
*	7	*	*	*	*	*	*	*
*	*	7	6	*	*	*	*	*
*	*	*	14	*	*	*	*	*
*	*	*	*	*	*	8	*	*

are the focal point of their lives as they strive to juggle them well. Accordingly, being able to deal with reality, adjusting to the lifestyle they have, and enjoying the moment are more important than contemplating existential questions such as meaning of life.

Tomohisa (2010) posited that there are two types of life struggles. One is a quotidian type including relationships at work, financial issues, family problems, and so forth; they are all personal struggles that people try to solve in order to have a better life. Another type of struggle is a more profound one that only religion could solve. For this younger and least religious group of people, religious matters and psychological well-being were not strongly associated with psychological health, possibly because the majority of them tend to focus on the first type of life struggles.

3.2 People with Moderate Religion-Related Experiences

A) *All-boys Catholic and all-girls middle/high school and all-girls Protestant middle/high school students*

Eight hundred forty-five all-boys Catholic middle and high school students participated in this survey. The average age was 15.4 (SD=1.5). Keywords such as empathy and consideration for others appeared most frequently (113 words) followed by kindness and fun-loving (96 words). Examples were "considerate to others when talking," "being considerate and taking actions accordingly," and "being kind to others." What separates this group from the previous group was that this group generated many *religion-related* keywords. Examples were "being able to live by the teachings of the Bible" or "believing in Jesus Christ." Although it is possible for middle/high school students to be concerned about religious matters in and of themselves, I believe that through religious education they were encouraged to think of a person with Christian faith as an ideal figure, which then becomes incorporated as their own image of psychological health.

In addition, 961 all-girls Catholic middle and high school students participated in this survey. The average age was 14.9 (*SD*=1.5). The result was similar to that of Catholic boys in that keywords of empathy and consideration for others appeared the most (479 words) followed by being kind and gentle. Examples were "paying attention to what others are going through and acting it as if it were one's own concern," "lending a helping hand when others are in need," and "being able to show kindness to others." Religion-related keywords were also extracted from phrases such as "being a god-like person" or "being able to deeply treasure oneself and the other."

For all-girls Protestant middle and high school students, the survey was collected at two different locations. At one school, 573 students participated with an average age of 14.5 years (SD=1.4). At another school, 463 students participated with an average age of 15.9 years (SD = 0.9). Thoughtfulness, empathy, and gentleness were the most frequently extracted keywords from phrases like "those who help others regardless of their own troubles" and "those who can experience others' joy and sadness." Religion-related keywords were also extracted from phrases such as "believing in the teachings of the Bible," "someone like Jesus Christ", and "somebody like a pastor." Interesting keywords such as forgiving were also observed.

In summary, there was an increase in numbers of keywords related to Christianity and/or the Bible when thinking about a psychologically healthy person. This is probably the result of religious education that these students receive at school.

B) *Religion-affiliated university students (Buddhist, Catholic, and Protestant)*

One hundred nineteen Buddhism-affiliated University students (87 men and 32 women, average age=19.7, SD=1.8), 896 Catholic University students (313 men, 577 women, and 6 N/A gender, average age=19.3, SD=1.4), and 377 Protestant University students (217 men, 158 women, and 2 N/A, average age=20.2, SD=2.1) participated in this study.

In this group, empathy, thoughtfulness, friendliness, and generosity were the top keywords. Examples included "those who can truly be happy for others," "being able to think for others," and "being able to accept others as who they are." It is noteworthy that more Christianity and religion related keywords were generated compared to those who attended the general universities and public middle and high schools. There are a few possible explanations for this result.

First, some students at the Protestant university were required to take a "Christian education" class, which could potentially influence how students conceptualize psychological health. Second, there were a number of students who reportedly were from either Christian or Buddhist families. Furthermore, college age is about the time when one starts contemplating existential issues (King & Roeser, 2009). In such a situation, a person often seeks guidance in the teaching of the Bible or Buddhist Scriptures in order to gain a peace of mind. Example phrases describing "psychologically healthy person" from these participants reflect this tendency: "those who know, to some extent, how to leave things to a higher power," "somebody who is perfect as a human being," and "someone who can show unconditional love to their family and others."

C) *Adult Catholics*

Since they are committed Christians, one can presume that people in this group have a fair amount of religious experiences which, in turn, should affect how they conceptualize psychological health. Seventy Catholics (28 men and 42 women) participated, and the average age was 61.0 (SD=15.1).

The most notable result was the high frequency of religion (Christianity)-related keywords (43 words) including "being able to pray for others whole-heartedly," "having faith and thanking God," "having serenity based on the Scriptures," "treating everyone equally with love." Other frequently generated keywords were empathy, thoughtfulness, self-sacrificial, and kindness (30 words). Specific phrases included "being able to treat the marginalized with warm welcome and care," "speaking and acting with consideration for others," "those without a selfish motive and desire." These results clearly reflect the saying in the Bible, "there is no greater love than to lay down one's life for one's friends."

Overall, for the adult Catholics, their lives are centered around the teaching of the Bible, and the ideal lifestyle is the one that reflects this teaching. Thus, the image of a psychologically healthy person is an ideal Christian who strives to lead a better life.

D) *Adult Protestants*

There were 763 participants (251 men, 497 women, 15 N/A) with the average age of 56.8 (SD=16.9). *Religion* (i.e., *Christianity*) *related* keywords were extracted the most (388 words). Examples included "loving neighbors," "unshakable faith," "surrendering to God," and "walking my life alongside of God." People also generated keywords empathy, thoughtfulness, self-sacrifice, and kindness (212 words) as well as forward-thinking, positive-thinking, and cheerful (152 words). Examples included "those who can give without thinking about one's own benefit," "always caring about other's wellness and happiness," and "being able to recover from disappointments." Although keywords related to empathy, thoughtfulness, self-sacrifice, and kindness were generated by both non-religious (general adults and non-religious university students) and the religious (the Catholics and the Protestants), this result should be interpreted with caution because, for the religious group the religion-related key words were most frequently generated followed by empathy, thoughtfulness, self-sacrifice, and kindness. In other words, for Christians, the empathetic and self-sacrificing characteristics were based on a more foundational Christian ideology, such as "Love thy neighbors."

In addition, generosity and fairness were also often generated keywords (e.g., "accepting, being comfortable with oneself, reliable, and independent") (124 words). Taken together, the Protestant participants seem to define a "psychologically healthy" person as a dependable leader who is firm in one's faith and always loving and accepting."

E) *Buddhists*/Soto *Buddhists*

One hundred sixty-five *Soto* Buddhists (98 men, 65 women, 2 N/A) participated in this survey (average age=60.9, SD=14.6). Empathy, thoughtfulness, self-sacrifice, and kindness (65 words) and forward-thinking, positive-thinking, and cheerful (26 words) were generated the most. Examples included "being empathetic and thoughtful of others," "putting other's needs before one's own," and "overcoming difficulties."

Another interesting finding was that they often referred to those keywords that were related to some of the fundamental Buddhist teachings (e.g., "not easily angered," "calmness, having a pacified mind, and peace of mind") (25 words). The phrases directly related to Buddhism such as "Buddha" and "seeking the truth" were also observed (13 words). It seems that their ideal image of a "healthy" person is someone who transcends daily disturbances such as anger and apprehension by following the path of Buddhism.

F) *New religion/Rissho-kosei-kai Buddhists*

Two hundred fifty-one *Rissho-kosei-kai* Buddhists (13 men, 232 women, 6 N/A) participated in this survey (the average age=62.8, SD=9.3). The most frequently referenced keywords were empathy, self-sacrifice, thoughtfulness, and serving others (120 words). Examples were "being empathetic towards others" and "taking care of others." Other keywords included kind, gentle, warm, forward-thinking, positive-thinking, and cheerful, and examples included "calm," "gentle," and "self-assured." Like people in other groups, these *Rissho-kosei-kai* participants conceptualized an ideal healthy person as someone who is empathetic, kind, and cheerful. In particular, they seemed to emphasize cherishing and serving others.

Further, as expected, people often generated religion-related (Buddhism) keywords, such as "those who feel the presence of Buddha and God in their minds," "people whose life is in accordance with the truth of the universe," and "people who look for inner peace in time of troubles." Not unlike the *Soto* Buddhists, these participants have a certain attitude towards their lives that revolve around Buddhist teachings.

G) *Shinto/Izumo-taisha Shintoists*

Forty-two *Izumo-taisha Shintoists* (12 men, 30 women, average

age=52.7, *SD*=15.5) participated. Although empathy and thoughtfulness (e.g., "someone who care for others," "a compassionate person") are often referenced, it was interesting to find that unlike other groups, these participants did not generate keywords related to self-sacrifice at all and only a few phrases related to kindness and gentleness. This may be due to the small sample size, however.

Further, phrases related to gratitude (e.g., "Constantly having a sense of gratitude" and "someone who is always grateful") and religion were often mentioned as well. They included "feeling God's intention in both good and bad times," "I feel I am kept alive," and *okage*. The notion of *okage* is noteworthy as it relates to the keyword "gratitude." Its literal meaning is shadow (*kage*) where invisible god(s) reside and watch over humans, and they in turn, are expected to appreciate the god(s) for keeping them alive. This sense of gratitude is linked to *Shintoism* in which mountains, rocks, the sun, and other inanimate objects were seen as embodiments of gods.

H) *Summary: People with moderate religion-related experiences*

A common trend in this group was the frequent reference to religion-related keywords. For the Protestant and Catholic Christians, "God," "faith" and "prayer" were frequently mentioned, indicating that their lives were firmly anchored in their faith. Onda (2010) defines prayer as "a means of communication with god(s), Buddha, holy beings, and/or supernatural beings." A Christian finds his or her path in life through prayer and by surrendering oneself to the all-transcending God.

Other religious groups also generated religion-related keywords although less frequently than the Christians. For the Buddhists, "psychologically healthy" implies those who are "calm" and transcend daily disturbances like being angry and impatient. For the *Shintoists*, on the other hand, a "psychologically healthy" person is appreciative of invisible gods, worships natural objects and phenomena as embodiments of gods while having a keen awareness that it is god(s) who keeps people alive.

Without referencing religion, the results thus far indicate that a "psychologically healthy" person for Japanese has empathetic, kind, forward-thinking, and cheerful characteristics. This image is consistent with that of Westerners (Oishi, 2006). With the religion-related keywords, the results reveal that people develop an ideal image of a psychologically healthy person in their respective faith traditions that surpasses common personality characteristics, and that suggests that humans have a potential to strive to become holy.

3.3 People with the Highest Religion-Related Experiences

Based on the results from the previous section with the members of five different religious organizations, we expected that religious leaders would generate more religion-related keywords. *Shinto* leaders were excluded from the following analyses due to the small sample size.

A) *Catholic leaders*

Sixty-six Catholic leaders (27 men, 38 women, 1 N/A) participated in this survey (average age=67.0, SD=15.9). Religion-related (Christianity) keywords were generated the most (34 words). Examples were "someone who lives with prayers and contemplation," "living a life with his or her soul soaring toward heaven and God," and "engaging with and smiling at people as if they were God." These phrases are a vivid portrayal of something sacred that is beyond the physical world and carry much more religious connotation than those generated by the organization members. Empathy, thoughtfulness, self-sacrifice, and kindness were also referenced frequently (34 words). Examples included "being able to look after others," "serving others," and "having a heart of empathy." Interestingly, both the Catholic members and the leaders frequently referenced the keywords associating helping and serving others, reflecting one of the core Christian teachings of "Love thy neighbors."

On the other hand, what distinguished the leaders from the church members were the keywords being independent and self-control, perhaps reflecting characteristics and skills necessary for the leaders. In summary, these Catholic leaders conceptualize "psychologically healthy" people as those who are deeply religious, yet cheerful and kind as leaders.

B) *Protestant leaders*

One hundred seven Protestant leaders (58 men, 48 women, 1 N/A, average age=58.2, *SD*=11.9) generated Religion-related (Christianity) keywords the most (105 words), including phrases like, "someone who always trusts in God who guides our path for the best," "someone who is devoted to God in both mind and body," and "somebody who is being healed by Christ's wounds."

What distinguished this group from the Catholic members and leaders as well as the Protestant members was that the second most frequently referenced keywords were not empathy, thoughtfulness, self-sacrifice, and kindness, but generosity, accepting, being comfortable with oneself, reliable and independent. Examples were "someone with peace of mind," "not easily swayed by situations," "trustworthy," and "having something unshakable." One possible explanation for this difference is the way the Protestant leaders live according to their faith. That is, their life revolves around cultivating a sense of independence, recognizing Christ as the cornerstone of the soul, and seeking Him with fervent enthusiasm.

In fact, keywords such as growth, effort, perseverance, and rising up were common for this group. The phrases associated with these keywords were "experiencing hardships but growing as a person despite despair and sadness" and "persevering patiently while experiencing oppression or pain," which all point to an image of someone who stands firmly on Christian faith all the while rising up against hardships in life. Yanaihara, a Japanese Christian scholar, listed three pillars of Christian life: faith, hope, and love. Of these three, Yanaihara (2012) explained hope as following (2012):

> *Christians are people of hope. No matter how miserable our life/world is, they are certain that with God, it could be overcome: and He will lead us to complete salvation… To live on this earth with this kind of hope is not a cowardly act as a way to escape from this world. Rather, this hope is the driving force to endure suffering, fearlessly fulfill the obligations of this world, and bravely fight the battle on this earth.*

The results for this group seem to reflect the concept of hope as proposed by Yanaihata. For this group, the image of "psychologically healthy" person is someone who is trustworthy, seeks God with fervor, bravely confronts many difficulties, and grows as a person.

C) *Soto Buddhism leaders*

Fifty *Soto* leaders (47 men, 3 women, average age=39.7, SD=10.8) participated in this survey. They generated religion-related (Buddhism) keywords the most (16 words). The phrases were mostly derived from the Buddhist teaching including "not easily provoked," "not easily disturbed by concerns," and "being able to process and analyze one's own emotional state." Some were more direct by saying things like "being like Buddha." The number of Religion-related (Buddhism) keywords were greater than that generated by the *Soto* Buddhism members, indicating the leaders' devotion.

Furthermore, equal numbers of phrases related to empathy, thoughtfulness, self-sacrifice, and kindness were generated such as "putting others before oneself," "understanding other's sadness," and "being considerate" (16 words). This image of someone who is self-disciplined while caring for and empathizing with others is consistent with the characteristics associated with Buddha. Thus, a "psychologically healthy" person for *Soto* Buddhist leaders is a kind, gentle, and self-disciplined holy person who has achieved enlightenment.

D) *Rissho-kosei-kai Buddhist leaders*

Fifty-eight *Rissho-kosei-kai* leaders (40 men, 18 women, average age=57.4, *SD*=5.7) participated in this survey. People generated keywords related to empathy, thoughtfulness, self-sacrifice, and kindness the most (46 words). Examples were "doing things for others," "cherishing the persons you hold dear," and "understanding others' feelings." This result is consistent with that of *Rissho-kosei-kai* members. Religion-related keywords came second (41 words). Sample phrases included "using pains or concerns for self-improvement," "accepting hardships as an opportunity for growth," and "recognizing everything as Buddha's mercy to improve oneself." These interpretations of psychological health are unique to this religious group. People, in general, try to avoid inconvenience, despair, and pain. Their teaching, however, encourages people to accept and find meanings in those hardships as Buddha would. It is a paradigm shift in which hardships in life were interpreted positively as an opportunity for growth. Moreover, I think that this perspective teaches people to look beyond the physical world, seeking Buddha's intention which, in turn, enables a person to communicate with the spiritual world.

As Shimai (2009) pointed out, according to World Survey of Happiness (Inglehart et al., 2008), people's happiness does not always positively correlate with materialistic wealth. This result indicates that material wealth may be necessary but not sufficient to fulfill our existential cravings. It is possible that the teaching of *Rissho-kosei-kai* provides its leaders and followers with a perspective that helps them find meanings in times of difficulties.

4. General Discussion

In the previous section, we presented the results of how religious leaders paint the image of "psychologically healthy" person. As expected, they all generated the largest number of religion-related keywords. Each group of religious leaders defined a "psychologically healthy" person as follows:

- Catholic and Protestant Christian leaders: A person who communicates with the holy, gains powers through prayer, and bravely confronts life's challenges.

- *Soto* Buddhism leaders: A calm and gentle person who is able to control emotional upsets like anger and fear.

- *Rissho-kosei-kai* leaders: A person who finds Buddha's intention in hardships and uses that opportunity for self-improvement and self-discovery.

There are differences and similarities among these religious groups in defining what constitutes psychological health. While those differences may stem from doctrines and teachings that are unique to each group, the concept of "growth" seems to be the common theme that weaves through the similarities (Haya, 2011). Here, "growth" implies a self-transformation in which a person discovers new and more profound perspectives so that he or she can accomplish what was impossible before.

From the results of the groups with minimum religious experience, one's psychological health and life concerns seem to have a negative correlation. That is, a person is psychologically healthy when his or her life concerns are diminished. As previously mentioned, there are two types of life concerns: concerns about daily life and existential matters (Tomohisa, 2010). While the former can be solved through counseling and other clinical treatments, existential concerns are often solved through religion.

Based on the result of this study, daily troubles we often encounter seem nested within the religious troubles, as the latter forces one to think critically about his or her life on a higher level. As we have discussed in this chapter, human growth means something beyond simple, physiological maturity. This concept of "growth" remains important as it opens up the possibility of making the world and oneself better, which is much like the self-actualization process that Maslow (1943) posited. This study revealed that religions could offer much to humans' trouble-filled lives, leaving plenty of room for more discussion on how religion could contribute to humans' psychological health. This supports Nakao's (2012) claim that having contact with religion, especially in contemporary Japan, may potentially give people a way to answer some of the most difficult questions in life.

5.

Finding Religion in Nature:
An Alternative Index of Religiosity

Ryo Nishiwaki, Nanzan University

Aside from various methodologies and types of analysis, one of the difficulties of studying religion from a psychological perspective is to articulate what religion means, especially to the researchers themselves. For the purpose of this chapter, my working definition of religion is, "Any human activity which pursues an answer for the ultimate questions of life undertaken while being aware of infinity beyond human existence and recognizing the relation between the self and this infinity" (Nishiwaki, 2004). In the study of the psychology of religion, it is presumed that religion is an integral aspect of a psychological experience that interacts with the outer world, and these interactions manifest themselves as religious beliefs and behaviors (see Introduction). Hence, even in our attempt to investigate religiosity among the general public (e.g., Japanese society), the focus must remain on the personal experience of each individual.

People, at some point in their lives, encounter the ultimate questions of life. P. Gauguin's well-known painting, titled "Where Do We Come From? What Are We? Where Are We Going?" is a response to this question. A sense of religiosity emerges as we painstakingly seek the answer by locating where we stand in the world. We must dialogue with "the other" and continue to explore who we truly are, as there is no "right" answer to such questions. Thus, religiosity is a process whereby one seeks to find where and who he or she is in a ternary relationship (self-others-world), because learning about others and the world is the ultimate way to learn about oneself.

How, then, can we assess religiosity? According to the definition employed in this chapter, the essence of one's religiosity emerges when an individual experiences religion first-hand. The challenge is that commonly used survey questions, such as "Do you believe in a certain religion?" or "Do you have faith in a certain religion?" clearly lack some critical, epistemological perspectives. Those questions are insufficient indices for learning about people's religious experiences as a psychological phenomenon (also see Prologue).

In order to fill in some of these gaps, this study looked at people's experience in nature as an alternative way to understand religiosity. Strangely, religious experience in nature has never been a popular topic, despite its long history as a subject of many other fields of studies. In this chapter, we shed light on the relationship between the self and the outer world in ternary relationships, revealing a new aspect of religiosity among the Japanese.

1. Are We Measuring What We Want to Measure? – Validity of Religiosity Indices

1.1 Are Japanese Faithful to "Don't Know" Religion?

The Japanese people are internationally known as "non-religious." In fact, many national survey results regarding people's affiliation with religious groups, faith in a certain religion, or their concept of gods and Buddha reveal that Japanese people are non-religious. A series of cross-cultural international surveys on religiosity also reveal that Japanese people, on average, show little interest towards religion. Their rating patterns are often characterized by "Don't know" answers, as Hayashi (1996) has pointed out.

In World Value Survey (2016),[1] for example, 53.3% answered that they do not have an affiliation with any religious groups (5th highest among 50 participating countries), and 6.3% did not answer the question (the highest among 50 countries) (Q43). To the question (Q46) "Regardless of your attendance at religious services, do you consider yourself religious?" 17.9% answered "Don't know," which ranked Japan as the highest, six points higher than the second country. To the question (Q47) "Do you believe in the existence of the things listed below?" 31.2% answered "Don't know" regarding the existence of god, and 40.2% did the same regarding the existence of hell. Japan ranked the highest for both, 15.4 points and 20.4 points higher than the second respectively. The rate of "Don't know" answers was uniquely high across all survey questions, which only gives us an obscure idea about what Japanese people think about religion. As strange as it may seem, on the surface, it may look like most Japanese people believe in the religion of "Don't know."

1.2 Religious Perspectives on Nature as an Alternative Index of Religiosity

This does not imply that the "Don't know" answers have no value or that Japanese people have no religion. In fact, it is quite the opposite. We need, however, to reevaluate the traditional indices for religiosity. In other words, questions regarding one's faith in institutionalized religion or people's concepts of god(s) or Buddha may not sufficiently measure their religiosity.

The recent discussion in the field of religious studies raises a further question on the meaning of religion among the Japanese. Ama (1996), for one, proposed that Japanese people's "non-religiousness" only reflects a lack of interest in organized religion, but not in a cherished faith which has been passed down from generation to generation. Similarly, Shimada (2009) explored the implications of their "non-religiousness," while Noelke (2014) pointed out Japanese people's high religiosity in their daily practices. Thus, the conventional ideas on religiosity do not sufficiently capture the religiosity of the Japanese.

What, then, could possibly capture such an elusive concept of Japanese religiosity? The conventional indices used in research may not be valid, and that is why the Japanese often respond with "Don't know" or "No religion." I propose using their attitudes toward nature as a novel index of religiosity. These are thoughts and feelings often evoked by nature. In order to better understand Japanese people's religiosity in their own cultural context, this study highlights people's psychological experience in nature and its impact on their self-perception.

2. Religious Perspectives on Nature
2.1 Why Nature?

Nature evokes various emotions in us. The beauty of nature touches our hearts, bringing awareness to our surroundings. Many of these feelings and experiences can be labeled "religious," as has been the case for many years not just in Japan, but throughout human history. All things that exist in nature, natural phenomena, and natural scenery have always been the subjects of worship. Their divine existence provokes a sense of awe. Thus, it seems only logical to find the source of religiosity in the experience of nature. By measuring a person's religiosity from this perspective, it allows us to 1) be grounded in the origin of human religiosity, and 2) investigate religiosity in a new light without the limit that conventional, institutionalized religions set in understanding the concept of spiritual matters.

A) *Previous studies*

As far as Japanese psychological studies are concerned, there are only a very few surveys on Japanese people's religious awareness that included items related to experience in nature. However, there is no study that specifically examined people's psychological experience in nature or focused on nature's psychological impact. Seki's (1944) large-scale survey research before WWII on children's religious awareness and behaviors is one of the few studies of this topic. In his survey, he specifically asked about their admiration for and perceptions of the sun and moon, as well as sentiments about "night" and "fire." Interestingly, he conceptualized certain scenes as "compound phenomena" where both natural and artificial things coexist. Examples included the scenery of a graveyard and the evening scenery of a large bell at a Buddhist temple (see Figure 5.1 and Figure 5.2). He concluded that "Natural and 'compound phenomena' such as stars, the ocean, rivers, lakes, mountains, forests, fields, old trees, the vast sky, and old battle fields as well as old castles often evoke religious sentiment as well as religion-related emotions" (Seki, 1944, p. 443). Emotions aroused by experiencing nature include "moral emotions" (gratitude, compassion, reminiscence, aversion, affection, etc.), "sacred emotions" (solemnity, stillness, desolation, fear, etc.) and "fearful emotions" (admiration, devoutness, submissiveness, reverence, etc.) (p. 450).

In studies from abroad, Hardy (1979) claims that people's experience in nature acts a significant trigger for the emergence of a person's religiosity. Sir Alister Hardy, a distinguished former marine biologist, conducted an extensive survey and collected anecdotes on people's religious experience, which he then organized and analyzed. The result showed that experiencing nature's beauty was ranked third as a significant religious experience followed by experiencing "depression and despair" and "prayer and meditation." For example, one participant reported that "I cannot help but worship whenever I encounter the beauty of nature." Hardy merely intended to investigate people's religious experience, but found out that experience in nature was one of the important elements of religiosity.

B) *Previous research (Japanese philosophy)*

Although psychological studies of nature and religion may be scarce, the significant role that nature has played in Japanese religious awareness has been focused upon in the field of the history of Japanese philosophy. Ienaga (1943) coined the term "Religious Perspectives on Nature," introducing the idea into the history of Japanese philosophy. He presented an overview of the religious functions that nature played from ancient time to modern days, with an emphasis on the Heian Era (AD8~AD12), claiming that, "The role nature played in our ancestors' spiritual life is similar to that of a savior in the institutionalized religions" (1997, p. 80). Examples include "the philosophy of the mountains" in which people sought salvation by staying away from cities and living in rural mountain heights, or "the philosophy of supernatural nature" in which people considered nature as "a symbol of sacredness as well as eternity, which transcends observables" (p. 115).

Aesthetician Ohnishi (1948) defined "emotions toward nature" as "our instantaneous psychological reaction to nature's scenery and phenomena" and classified them into six types. "Religious emotion toward nature" is one of these emotions, and it entails a sentiment towards nature derived from one's devotion to a religion. In the West, this particular type is strongly tied to the idea of Creationism, which considers nature as a divine symbol or God's creation. On the other hand, in the East, including Japan, this type of emotion is implicated in the dialectic notion of void, or a pessimistic and an escapist view of life that allows people to avoid, at least at the emotional level, an inevitable confrontation with nature.

Further, Ohnishi points out a fundamental difference between Japan and the West regarding how a sense of aesthetics relates to the religious emotions toward nature. In the West, an aesthetic sense is structured as an additional element of religious emotion toward nature, thus requiring a person to express his or her aesthetic experience in nature as a religious experience. The opposite is true in Japan. The religious emotion toward nature is the additional element to the sense of aesthetics, thus allowing one to use aesthetic expression to describe his or her religious experiences.[2]

Figure 5.1 *A large bell at a Buddhist temple. https://photo.pocket-free.net*

Figure 5.2 *A traditional graveyard. Photo by Takara Shashin-kan*

2.2 Basic Frameworks

In the following, I will discuss 1) the framework of people's perception as well as emotions during their encounter with nature, and 2) the definition of such perception and emotions.

In our study, we defined "religious perspective on nature" as "perception and emotions during our encounter with (or an exposure to) nature" (Ienaga, 1997, 1943). Although "perspective on nature" generally implies a perception only toward nature itself, here I use the term as having two senses: the perception toward nature itself and the realization of self-existence as a result. When we encounter nature, our responses may be, "What great scenery," or "I feel like there is divinity in this nature." However, we might also respond in this way, "I feel so small standing in the midst of this vast nature." In this case, the first half is the perception of nature, and the latter half is the realization of self-existence. The figure 5.3 depicts the mechanism behind this two-tiered process. For example, when *Saigyo*, a well-known Buddhist monk in the *Heian* era visited the Grand Shrine at *Ise* located in the middle of an ancient forest, he composed a poem, "I don't know who is out there looking after us, but I'm moved to tears because I feel so blessed" (Figure 5.4). Here, his perception of nature (A) is accompanied with the realization of self-existence

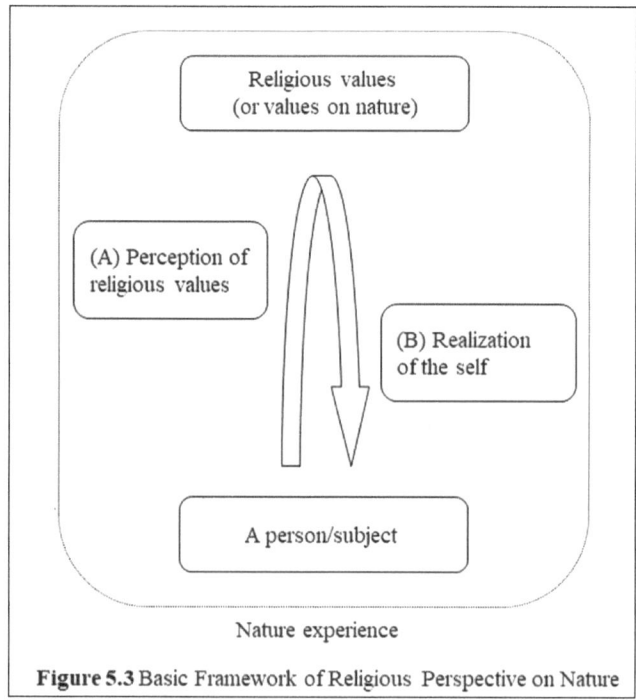

Figure 5.3 Basic Framework of Religious Perspective on Nature

Figure 5.4 *The Grand Shrine at Ise. https://www.tokyo-date.net*

(and awe) (B). In other words, a realization of the self is an essential part of religiosity. In sum, "the religious perspective on nature" has both observational and introspective aspects, which inevitably involve not only cognitive realization but also an emotional reaction.

2.3 Aspects of "Religious Perspective on Nature"

I defined "Religious perspective on nature" in the previous section, but the question remains, what exactly constitutes this concept. I propose a few possible aspects of this ancient, yet new concept in Table 5.1. Please note that these aspects are meant to be broad and non-exhaustive, because such a complex and elusive concept associated with the human psyche should be flexible and leave plenty of room for further interpretation.

Table 5.1 Religious Perspective on Nature (Contents)

The subject of religious values
(1) Expressions used to describe existence
(e.g., God, gods, Buddha, spirit, souls)
(2) Expressions used in describing values
(e.g., The Almighty, Supreme Being, Supernatural beings, Life, Eternity, Infinity)
Introspection and associated emotions
(1) Realization of self-existence
(e.g., Finiteness of individual existence, Helplessness, Joy of living, Healing of the self through nature)
(2) Religious emotions
(e.g., Awe, Mystery, Gratitude, Humility, Repentance)

Nishiwaki (2004)

3. The Religious Mind Experiencing Nature: Research on Religious Perspective on Nature
3.1 Method

As a part of J-MARS, we created a brief scenario of someone's experience in nature and an open-ended question which contained two aspects of religious perspective on nature: 1) the observation of life ("the grasses and wild flowers are full of life") and 2) subsequent introspection that accompanied a reference to one's smallness and helplessness ("What a small thing I am…").

The paragraph below is a short report of someone's experience in nature. If you have ever experienced something similar, please check "Yes." Then, write down your experience in the following section. If "No," you may skip to the next question.

> *I went hiking to a nearby mountain with my friend. The light-colored cherry blossoms were in full bloom, and clouds were floating in a vast blue sky. As we watched this relaxing scenery, a thought came into my mind: "What a small thing I am compared to this!" I then shifted my eyes and noticed that the grasses and wild flowers are full of life.*

- Have you ever experienced something similar (not limited to mountains)?
  ☐ Yes   ☐ No

- Please write down your experience.

It requires some explanation as to why smallness and helplessness were used as an introspective sentence. In Nishiwaki's (2004) study, participants reported their "religious experience," which was defined as "a description of experience in nature by which a person contemplates one's own existence and the continuity between the self and-nature (irrespective of references to the existence of gods, Buddha, the soul, etc.)." While there were four introspective categories related to religious experience (including "the mystery of existence," "the joy of existence"), "smallness and helplessness" seemed to be the best representation, as it was most frequently mentioned, and it straightforwardly expresses the respondents' sentiments on an existential question. Examples of "smallness and helplessness" included, "I felt small," "I was just a tiny thing," or "I learned that humans are helpless."

3.2 Results and Discussion
A) *Descriptive statistics*

Table 5.2 shows the basic data about whether or not four groups (middle school students, high school students, university students, and adults/believers/religious leaders) have had similar religious experiences in nature. Table 5.3 shows the distribution of only middle school and high school students who responded "yes." Among college students ($n = 1{,}531$; 56.3% women, 43.2% men), 58.5% were Catholics, 26.6% Protestants, 7.8% Buddhists, and 9.1% identified as "other". Among the adults/believers/religious leaders ($n = 1{,}754$; 62.9% women, 35.6% men), 43.5% were Protestants, 6.1% Protestant leaders, 14.3% Risshokouseikai, 3.3% Risshokouseikai leaders, 9.4% *Soto* Buddhists, 2.9% *Soto* Buddhism leaders, 4.0% Catholics, 3.8% Catholic leaders, 2.4% Izumo *Shintoists*, and 0.7% Izumo *Shinto* leaders, and 9.7% identified as "other."

Table 5.2 Results of Religious Perspective on Nature

	With experience		Without experience (%)	NA (%)
	n	%		
Middle school students ($n = 1{,}637$)	485	29.6	65.1	5.3
High school students ($n = 1{,}691$)	505	29.9	65.6	4.5
University students ($n = 1{,}531$)	495	32.3	66.6	1.0
Adults, believers, and religious leaders ($n = 1{,}754$)	1,133	64.6	29.0	6.4

	Rate of religious perspective on nature in the answers "with experience"					
	1. Smallness and helplessness	1 and 3	2. Recognition of living things	2 and 3	3. Both	Others
Middle school students ($n = 485$)	28.5	35.1	13.8	20.4	6.6	51.1
High school students ($n = 505$)	24.8	26.8	7.1	9.1	2.0	66.1
University students ($n = 495$)	37.0	39.2	7.3	9.5	2.2	53.5
Adults, believers, and religious leaders ($n = 1{,}133$)	20.6	24.5	13.5	17.5	4.0	62.0

Table 5.2 shows that in all three younger age groups, middle school, high school and university students, approximately 30% reported that they have a similar experience while 65% did not. This is particularly important, given that only less than 5% of the students reported a similar experience in Nishiwaki's (2014) study when a brief anecdote was not provided.

Table 5.3 Details of Participants of Middle/High School Students

Participants of middle school students ($n = 1,637$)	n	%
All-girls Catholic middle school	579	35.4
All-boys Catholic middle school	454	27.7
All-girls Protestant middle school (A)	370	22.6
All-girls Protestant middle school (B)	145	8.9
Public middle school (47 boys, 39 girls, and 3 non-respondents)	89	5.4
Participants of high school students ($n = 1,691$)	n	%
Public high school (211 boys, 180 girls, and 6 non-respondents)	397	23.5
All-boys Catholic high school	391	23.1
All-girls Catholic high school	382	22.6
All-girls Protestant high school (B)	318	18.8
All-girls Protestant high school (A)	203	12.0

In junior high school students, boys account for 30.6% and girls account for 69.2%. In high school students, boys account for 35.6% and girls account for 64.0%.

In an older age group, approximately 60% of adults/believers/religious leaders reported that they had a similar experience. This result may indicate a positive relationship between age and the acquisition of religious perspective on nature, although such a conclusion may be premature, as our older sample was comprised of either believers or religious leaders.

Among those who had similar experiences, more participants responded with references to existential insight (e.g., "smallness and helplessness" of oneself) than those referring to "recognition of living things" (See section 3.1 in this chapter or Table 5.1). On another note, more than half of the participants responded with sentences that do not refer to either existential insight or recognition of living things. In other words, the study generated relatively diverse responses despite the fact that an anecdotal scenario was presented, which usually brings people's attention to the themes included in the story.

B) *Details of gaining "Religious perspective on nature"*

In the following, I will focus on the results of the youngest age groups, i.e. middle school and high school students. This age group has particularly important developmental implications because, unlike the older participants who gave quite stereotyped responses, these adolescents tend to describe their experience simply and intuitively (Table 5.4).

Five sub-groups were identified within this group: (1) Those who had a similar experience but did not provide any description; (2) Those who had a similar experience with only a description of a situation; (3) Those who had a similar experience with a description of the situation but simply agreeing with the reaction described in the scenario (e.g., "I felt the same way as described in the anecdote"); (4) Those who had a similar experience but the description was not directly related to nature (e.g., "I gained such a perspective while watching a film" or "while I was on a train"); and finally (5) Those who had a similar experience and described the situation and their reaction to it. Among those five groups, (1), (2) and (3), which do not include any description of their experience, are not suitable for the analysis given the purpose of this study. The same applies to group (4), since the description provided did not focus on the topic that this study intended to examine. Thus, the following analysis only concerns group (5).

Table 5.4 Middle/High School Students With Similar Experiences
990 middle/high school students
(485 middle school students and 505 high school students)

	n	%
1. No description	99	10.0
2. Similar experience/Not agreeing	80	8.1
3. Similar experience/Agreeing	72	7.3
4. Description without nature	165	16.7
5. Similar experience/Original description	574	58.0
[Details]	[n]	[%]
Existential realization	262	45.6
Recognition of living things	103	17.9
Both	42	7.3
Others	167	29.1

C) *Findings from answers to open-ended questions*

A total of 990 middle school and high school students responded that they had experiences in nature similar to those suggested in the survey. 58% (574 out of 990) described their own experience in nature with sentences related to the associated perception and feelings. Using the KH Coder, a text-mining software, I examined the relationship between words that appeared in a similar pattern (Higuchi, 2014). This was limited to nouns (excluding proper nouns such as names of specific groups, people, and places), verbs, adjectives and adverbs, which appeared at least ten times (i.e. if a word appeared less than nine times, it was eliminated from the subsequent analysis), Figure 5.5 shows 30 word-pairs with 33 words (*density* = .057). The size of the circles indicates the frequency of the word's appearance, and the thickness of the lines indicates the strength of the relationship.

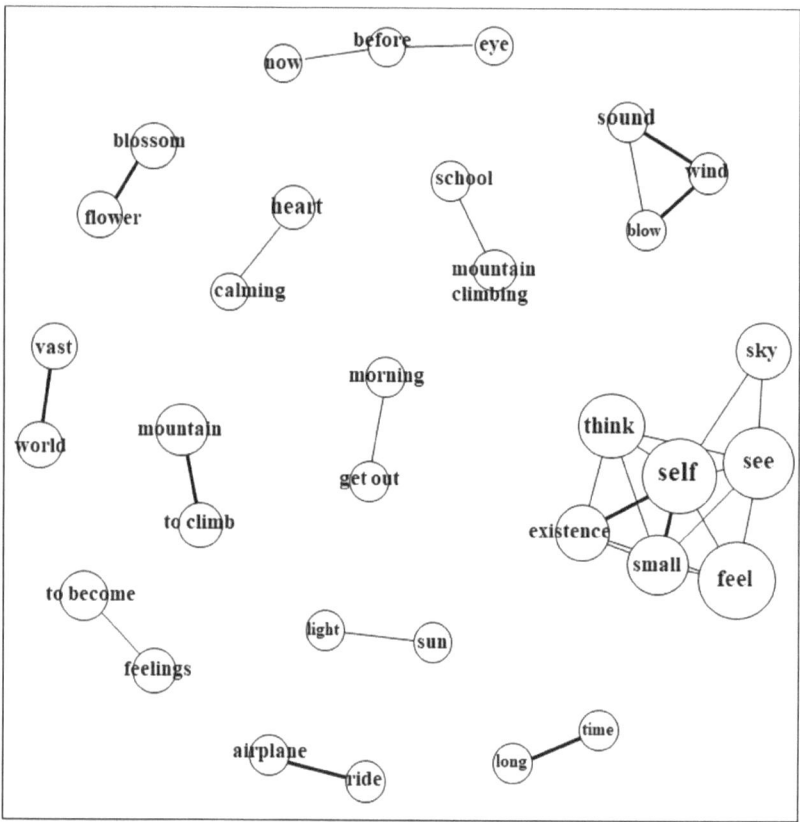

Figure 5.5 - The Relationship of Words Based on Experiences in Nature

On the right side of Figure 5.5, there is a cluster, consisting of seven words, in which the pair of "self" and "small," as well as the pair "self" and "existence" have a strong relationship. This particular cluster indicates that there are many sentences such as, "I felt my existence was small when I looked up at the sky." Those words characterize a prototypical religious perspective where one becomes aware of self-existence in nature. There are a total of 12 other clusters which include 3-words clusters with words such as "sound," "wind," and "blow," or 2-words cluster with words such as "flower" and "bloom," "mind" and "calm," or "vast" and "world." These results show that the participants frequently men-

114

tioned different aspects of nature (i.e., "flowers bloom," "wind blows" or "sound of winds," and "sunshine"), the situations in which the experience occurred (i.e., "mountain climbing on a school trip," "riding on airplane," and "climbing mountains"), and the contents of the experience ("calming mind"). Interestingly, even though many participants reported visual features of nature, some mentioned an auditory aspect of their experience (e.g., "sound-blow-wind"), indicating the use of various senses in experiencing nature.

D) *Recognizing the existential question*

304 students, classified in group (5) shown in Table 5.4, described their experience with both introspective (realization of the existential question) and observational (recognition of living things) sentences. In this group, "smallness" of one's existence was often mentioned (see descriptions 1 through 4). Although the use of the word, "small" in the brief prompt provided in the survey may have influenced participants' choice of words, other words with a similar nuance, such as "helplessness" or "uncertainty," also appeared frequently. In many cases, the visible contrast between vast nature and the small self seems to trigger this existential question; however, some clearly understood that there was something more than the visual, physical differences between people and nature (see Description 3). Given this result, the comments about "smallness and helplessness," triggered by visible impressions, imply the adolescents' realization in terms of where they stand in the context of the outer world. Further, descriptions 4 and 5 are good examples of the cases in which these adolescents came up with the existential questions and, as a result, began thinking deeply about their lives.

> **Description 1:** *On my way home from school, I looked up, and the sky was clear with little clouds. Looking at that sky, I felt the smallness of my existence. I don't know why, but it almost made me cry. (7th grade, girl)*

> **Description 2:** *It was a family trip to Hokkaido. Unlike the cramped quarters of cities with skyscrapers, I felt the closeness of magnificent, mysterious nature. Then I realized how uncertain my existence was. (7th grade, girl)*

Description 3: *When I climbed Mt. Fuji, I felt a difference, beyond that of physical size, between the mountain and humans. I came to understand that was the root of nature worship in ancient Japan. (11th grade, boy)*

Description 4: *When I look up at the night sky, I think of my existence. Compared to the scale of the universe, I feel so small and it made me wonder about why I am alive." (11th grade, boy)*

Description 5: *There is lots of nature nearby my house, and the air is very clear. Spring, summer, autumn, and winter— all year around, when I look up, the view is never the same, but always changing. At night, the moon and the stars shine beautifully. When I watch them, I think that my life is short, and it makes me ponder my own existence. (9th grade, girl)*

Such introspective processes occur after the observation of nature. Some only described a simple realization of one's smallness without evaluating it, while others, although the numbers were fewer, described it with either a positive or negative evaluation of their own existence. There were seven descriptions with positive evaluations, and five descriptions with negative evaluations. The example descriptions are below.

Description 6: *During a family trip, I was looking up the cloudless blue sky while floating on the clear ocean. Then I thought of my trivial existence within this whole universe, but I also thought that it has been a good life. (8th grade, girl).*

Description 7: *When I went mountain climbing with my family, I felt that my existence was so uncertain that I could vanish at any given time. (9th grade, girl)*

Description 8: *When looking at a star that exists millions of light-years away, it makes me feel that my existence does not matter. (11th grade, girl)*

Description 6 positively evaluates her life as a good one, despite the smallness she felt in nature. Description 8, on the other hand, negatively evaluates her existence as "...does not matter." These results reveal the ambivalent feeling toward one's life common among adolescents, constantly swinging between "worthy" and "unworthy" in order to find out who they are vis a vis the larger world.

4. Conclusion

In this study, nearly 30% of middle school and high school students and about 60% of adults, including believers and religious leaders, responded as having had an experience similar to the one described in the survey, and as a result, had gained a religious perspective on nature. Among middle and high school students who responded that they had a similar experience, about 50% posed existential questions to themselves. The purpose of this study was to challenge the conventional idea of religiosity and to propose a "religious perspective on nature" as an alternative index of religiosity. In particular, this study makes a significant contribution to the on-going discussion of religiosity in the field of psychology by presenting empirical data.

In recent years, spirituality, as distinct from institutionalized religiosity, has emerged as a key concept (King & Boyatzis, 2015); it is more compatible with the "religious perspective on nature" as it does not overlap with pre-existing religions. In other words, "religious perspective on nature" more readily allows researchers to explore spirituality from what may be a developmental perspective. I hope to see future studies which provide a better understanding of human religiosity and spirituality.

Notes:

[1] World Value Survey is an international collaborative survey administered by social scientists in each country. Its head quarter is in Stockholm, Sweden. The latest data as of January 2016 (the 6th survey project) are posted on http://www.worldvaluessurvey.org.

[2] For example, the most recent Government Curriculum Guidelines in ethics instruct the elementary and junior high school teachers that the students should develop a sense of awe and inspiration toward something that is "beautiful" (aesthetics) and "beyond human power" (religious value).

6.

Hidden *Shinto* Narrative in Japanese Culture: A Religion that is Too Ubiquitous

Katsuya Sakai, Izumo Shrine Yawaragi Branch

1. The Beginning – Narrative Psychology Meets *Shintoism* (Figure 6.1)

Figure 6.1 *Izumo Grand Shrine. https://pixabay.com/ja/*

Why me? Why is it that I am the only one who has to go through hardships? I just don't understand. There must be no gods or Buddha.

As a director of a *Shinto* shrine in Tokyo, I also work as a priest and as a counselor. I have heard these phrases countless times from my clients. I used to try my best to answer these questions by providing "facts" or explanations of causes and effects of their situations, hoping that this would convince them to accept things as they are. However, when I came across the idea of "narratives" used in therapeutic situations, it became clear that what I was doing was far from being therapeutic.

Based on Social Constructionism, McNamee and Gergen (1992/1997) posited that our general understanding of "accurate" and "objective" truth about nature or oneself is merely a social production. Rather than looking at scientific knowledge as a rational, superior one, the concept of narrative allows us to capture human knowledge as cultural and historical processes where certain perspectives become dominant while suppressing others. In light of this account, my attempts at answering clients' questions about "why" bad things happen clearly failed to meet their expectations. What those clients needed was not the actual reason or the facts that underlay the problem—rather, it was their own "narrative" that they were seeking that would make sense for them.

Morioka (2008) and others point out that in a modern information society, interpersonal relationships have been weakened due to the increase of the multi-media use which requires less face-to-face interaction. Scientifically proven "treatment" no longer works as a broad cure in this complex, pluralistic society. As a result, it has become evident that conventional scientific methods have failed to capture the meanings behind human activities. The concept of narratives may answer the question of how people live their lives and why they do so, restoring human knowledge into the work of clinical science grounded in actual human experience.

One's worldview, value system, identity, perception of the reality, common sense and morals can be all explained within the framework of socially constructed narratives. When they all harmonize and orchestrate a grand story of "life," one may feel happy. But when something goes wrong and brings a note of dissonance, the whole story loses its shape and unity, causing a person to suffer, to be irritated, and to feel depressed. As Bruner (1990/1999) mentioned, people naturally seek meaning and values even in very insignificant matters. Referring to a client's claim that things were beyond her understanding, suggestions such as, "you can stay positive if you change the way you perceive reality no matter the situation," or "you have to focus on good things that happened despite the current situation," did nothing for the client as she found no meaning or value in them. Clients who come in with their concerns seek an explanation that fits into their own stories. It goes without saying that there is no "right" or "wrong" answer to those "why" questions. The answers are numerous and unique to every single client who seeks them.

> *Why me? Why is it that I am the only one who has to go through such hardships?*

This client described her life story full of abusive relationships and misfortunes. She was abused by her parents and then by her husband, and eventually lost her only child. Struggling to find something to say, I finally brought up the word "god," stating that there might be god's intension behind these things, from which she could learn so that her soul would grow and mature as a result.

> *That may be so.*

She said, after a long pause with a soft smile. Then, she went on and shared another story. When she tried to hang herself, the picture of her late child sprang up before her eyes and brought her back to reality, which, kept her from committing suicide. She said, "God might be telling me that I still had a mission to complete on this earth." Although she did not share too much more that day, she left my office with a sense of determination on her face. A year later, I received an email from her, thanking me for the time we talked and reporting that she was blessed with a good workplace and that things were going well. It seemed as if she had found a way to transform her story into one that makes sense to her, and had regained purpose back into her life.

Having encountered many instances where people's life stories gets restored through religious accounts, I came to understand religion as narratives that are intricately woven into one's life. This chapter aims to provide the basis for this hypothesis in the context of *Shintoism* in Japan by showcasing ideas and phrases that are culturally prominent. I then illustrate the results of the current study composed of questionnaires as well as a series of interviews on how *Shinto* believers experience god's blessings, particularly on the topic of matchmaking, the best known benefit of *Shintoism*.

2. The Roots of *Shintoism* and the Master Narrative of the Japanese

The concept of "narrative" has long been discussed in various settings including clinical or medical practices. In the field of psychology, Yamada (2000) explains the narrative as a nestled structure. The figure 6.2 shows that in our society, the narrator and the audience construct the story together as a cooperative action under the influence of the situational context (i.e., the present ambience, interpersonal relationships) as well as cultural, societal context (i.e., traditions, folklores, myths), which are nested within the historical (i.e., linguistic system) and ecological contexts (i.e., regional climate and natural features, physiological rhythms).

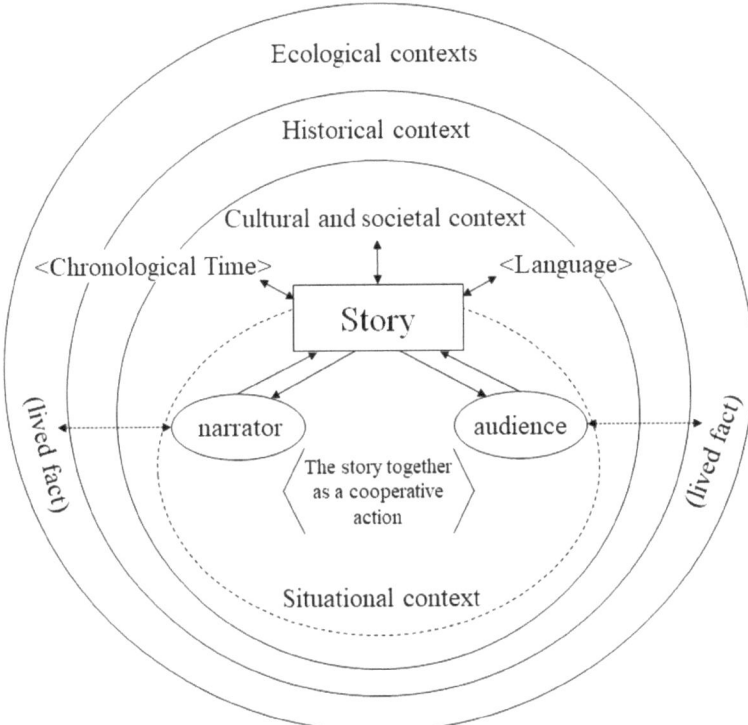

Figure 6.2 Cooperative Action by Story and Narrative (Yamada, 2000)

Religion seemingly has a similar structure, where various contexts intricately influence each other. The majority of what we perceive as "truth," "good," or "righteous" are simply the products of stories that people in the past created (McNamee & Gergen, 1992). Kawashima (2011) suggests that religion offers a way of life as well as "a template for the semantics of death" (p. 24) within a given socio-cultural context. That is, these stories are the "master narratives" that religions provide, which people perceive as "common sense." For the female client mentioned above, it is uncertain to what extent the narrative about god(s) that I introduced helped her in finding meaning in life. However, the god's story somehow resonated with her, and she was able reconstruct her own life story in a way that made sense to her.

No matter how we live or how we narrate our own stories, we are under the influence of such master narratives. Master narratives are so ingrained in the fabrics of our cultural psyche that we do not even recognize their existence. In this chapter, I intend to extract some of those master narratives that have been buried underneath the *Shintoism*-based cultural phrases and ideas that are common among the Japanese, which may even reveal the root of "the Japanese way of thinking."

2.1 *"Mizu ni Nagasu"* – The Narrative of "Let Bygones Be Bygones"

One of the most commonly used and well-known *Shinto* phrases is *Mizu ni Nagasu*, which literally translates "Letting it flush in water" (Figure 6.3). Its English equivalent would be something like "Let bygones be bygones." This phrase is particularly unique to Japan given its abundant water resources. Surrounded by water, the islanders, for centuries, have simply washed and cleaned their bodies and various items with water when they get dirty. Interestingly, this idea of cleansing was applied not only to a physical stain, but also to a psychological one. Whether it be a negative feeling, emotion, memory, experience or guilt, it can be washed and cleansed with water. *Misogi*, originated from "trimming back," exactly portrays this concept. It is an important *Shinto* ritual where a person can "trim back" his or her psychological stains that he or she picked up consciously or unconsciously along the way, by exposing oneself in water (e.g., under a waterfall or in the waves of the ocean) often in a form of meditation.

The idea of *Misogi* clearly derives from a belief that human nature is fundamentally good. People believe that "dirt" that became attached through daily activities can simply be removed by washing, implying the innate cleanness of human nature. According to the narrative perspective, this belief has become a master narrative as it has been widely shared among Japanese. In fact, this idea is such an integral part of *Shintoism* that all *Shinto* rituals start with *Shubatsu* (Purification) of the impure. According to the worldview of *Shintoism*, every person is a "child of god," and is born with a pure soul.

Figure 6.3 *Misogi*. Photo by Katsuya Sakai

A religious service called *Kounomachi* perfectly describes this *Mizu ni Nagasu* spirit (Figure 6.4). *Kounomachi* is an annual religious service held in Oiso-machi, Kanagawa Prefecture on May 5th, where all the *Mikoshi* (portable shrines) gather together from six different regions that once comprised the state of *Sagami*. During the service, a performance called *Za-mondo* takes place where all six shrines compete with each other by raising their tiger skin, which symbolizes power and authority, up towards the place of honor, in order to determine who is the most honorable and the highest of them all. In the middle of this performance, however, the *Shinto* priest who oversees and coordinates this ritual makes a claim in front of gods by saying, "A decision pending until next year!" The conclusion has been "flushed out" until "next year" every year, for over a thousand years. Although everyone technically knows which shrine holds the highest place among them, its honorable status is "on hold" until the decision is made, which, of course, is never.

As Kawashima (2011) pointed out, narratives include not only the contents expressed in a symbolic form (i.e., visual arts, performances, physical expressions, etc.), but also the actions that convey the contents. In this sense, *Shinto*'s performances and rituals that have been shared and practiced over hundreds and thousands of years are the very narratives that *Shintoism* offers. In the example of *Kounomachi*, some may criticize the ambiguity and procrastination at reaching the decision; however, the narrative that discourages quick decision-making and allows uncertainty may help prevent unnecessary competition and confrontation. Here, we can find the value of *Mizu ni Nagasu* spirit, which can be reiterated as a virtue deeply rooted in Japanese culture.

Figure 6.4 *Kounomachi in Oiso-machi, Kanagawa. Photo by Katsuya Sakai*

2.2 The Narrative of "Collectivism"

The second example is "Collectivism" (e.g., Markus & Kitayama, 1991; Singelis et al., 1995). Asoya (1994), for example, points out that Japanese culture has tendency to "emphasize the group rather than individuals" and a tendency to "value hard work (diligence)" (p. 33). According to Asoya (1994), these two features are closely related to traditional rice farming where the root of *Shintoism* philosophy can be found. In rice farming, it is imperative to have a community-wide irrigation system, and that practical fact did not leave any room for selfish individualism. Asoya (1994) claims that this mindset is the foundation of the Japanese collectivism, which eventually led to the stereotype of an interdependence and passivity that we see and hear of today. As Kaneko (1997) also points out, the master narrative described here is that group harmony needs to be preserved at all cost, and that there is a set of rules that one is expected to follow as a member of the group.

These dominant ideas that underlie *Shinto* narrative contrast sharply with the Western narratives that emphasizes autonomy and independence and a clear "psychological boundary" between self and others (Maruya, 1999).

What is important here is not to determine whether one narrative is more legitimate than the other. Instead, we must recognize why these cultural, historical differences exist and how we could construct a productive and complementary framework. This is why I am proposing to decipher the Japanese master narrative. Doing so may allow us to see our own religiosity and spirituality, despite our self-proclaimed "non-religiousness."

2.3 *Kotoage Sezu* – The Narrative of "Keeping It to Yourself"

The third example is one of many common *Shinto* phrases, *Kotoage Sezu* (Keeping it to yourself). Its literal translation is, "Do not say what you truly think." In *Kojiki,* the oldest existing Japanese history book (AD 712), one of the royals was cursed to death because he expressed his evil thoughts (Takeda & Nakamura, 1999). Similarly, in the *Manyoshu,* Japan's oldest poetry collection (8th century), Kakinomoto Hitomaro wrote, "A country filled with ears of rice, A country who obeys the gods, A country where no one says what they truly think, But I shall dare express my feeling regardless." This poem insinuates the virtue that many Japanese people cherish to this day – not uttering their true feelings or opinions.

Some commonplace cultural practices that illustrate this idea includes when Japanese people say, "This is nothing special," as they hand a gift to someone. No matter how much thought and money one invested in that gift, a Japanese person would not say, "This is a wonderful gift I picked just for you." Mihashi (2007) cites Fujitani Mitsue, a Japanese classical scholar in Edo period, and claims that Japanese people have developed a particular communication style where people say the opposite of what they actually think. Are Japanese people all liars? I do not think so. In one sense, it may be a strategic way to amplify the joy of the gift recipients by keeping their expectations low. Whatever the reasons for this traditional rhetoric, the master narrative of "Keeping it to yourself" encourages people not to say what they truly feel or think in order to communicate their true feelings to others in Japanese culture.

Further, it is interesting to note that even though true feelings and opinions are supposed to be kept to oneself, there is a particular time that is acceptable to utter what one really believes: When alone with god(s) for a time of prayer. Prayer is an essential part of many religions, of which *Shintoism* is not an exception. The Japanese word for prayer, *Inori,* consists of two segments; the first syllable "*I*" indicates god(s) while the latter half *nori* indicates *Kotoage.* In other words, praying in the world of *Shintoism* is equivalent to violating the sacred rule by saying what one truly feels, all the while being cleansed. There are many other *Shinto*-related words that begins with a sound of "*I*" indicating the existence of god(s) such as *Imigoto* (all *Shinto* rituals), *Inochi* (life), *Ine* (rice), *Iki* (breath), *Ikiru* (to live) (Mihashi, 2007; Tsuchihashi, 1990). In the earlier example of the traditional Japanese poems, the author *Kakinomoto Hitomaro* was willing to risk his life and break a taboo in order to tell his romantic interest how much he loves her. Here, we learn that this love letter was meant to prove his faithfulness and genuine feeling.

3. *En-Musubi* – The Narrative of "Matchmaking"

As a part of J-MARS project, we conducted a simple questionnaire regarding how *Shintoists* experience the merits of the deity. Twelve *Shinto* leaders from various ranks and 42 *Shinto* believers responded to the question, "Have you ever experienced the blessing of the deity (i.e., divine plan, guidance, signs, intervention, authority, protection)?" We originally planned a "Yes/No" binary question, followed by an open-ended question asking for more details. During a pilot interview, however, some *Shinto* leaders mentioned that they experience god's blessings rather vaguely, which makes it hard to come up with a concrete example. Based on this feedback, we decided to add, "I experience it subtly in daily life" as the third option. As it turned out, six *Shinto* leaders and 18 believers chose this third option, which was 50% and 42.9% of each group respectively. Five *Shinto* believers did not answer to the question possibly due to the difficulty in understanding the questions, unwillingness to take time to answer, or a psychological burden or guilt they might have felt by saying "No," especially to those in a leadership position with whom these participants talk face to face on regular basis. Since all narratives are under the influence of social circumstances such as this, future studies should take those situational contexts into considerations (Table 6.1).

Table 6.1 Experience of the Merits of the Deity

Deity	Shinto believers	Shinto leaders
Yes	8 (19.0)	6 (50.0)
Somewhat	18 (42.9)	6 (50.0)
No	11 (26.2)	0
NA	5 (11.9)	0
Total	42 (100.0)	12 (100.0)

The result also showed that 11 believers (26.2%) said they have never experienced the blessing of following the deity, but all the *Shinto* leaders have experienced them. Having been in a teaching position myself, it seems particularly clear that leaders tend to pay attention to how even a small daily event can be understood as a blessing of the deity. Providing a narrative that would help others to direct their lives towards the gods is an essential part of our job as *Shinto* leaders. Hence, it is only natural that a majority of the leaders responded that they "sense the blessings of the deity vaguely in my daily life." This seems to be the case especially when *Shinto* leaders teach people the idea of "*Yuuken Ichijyo*," which directs us to understand phenomena that occur in a tangible way in our real world as a reflection of the unseen gods' world and their intentions.

Among both leaders and believers combined, 14 people who have experienced the blessings of following the gods provided a total of 15 accounts. The open-ended question consisted of the following: 1) How old were you when the event took place? 2) When and how did it happen? 3) Please describe your experience in detail. Out of 15 accounts, six (40%) contained a "survival story" where people nearly died through car or water accidents ($n = 3$), overcame serious illnesses ($n = 2$), as well as a near-death experience ($n = 1$). Other accounts included "guidance experience (26.7%; $n = 4$)" where people had an audial or a visual guidance from gods, "match-making experiences (20%; $n = 3$)" where people were led to someone precious, "a sense of floating consciousness (6.7%; $n = 1$)," as well as "solution for a financial problem (6.7%; $n = 1$)."

Among those narratives, "a match-making experience" is one of the most well-known *Shinto* narratives (Figure 6.5). In fact, one of the main shrines, *Izumo-taisha,* celebrates a god of matchmaking. It is common for unmarried Japanese individuals to visit *Izumo-taisha* so that they could ask the god(s) for the matchmaking favor of finding a future spouse (Figure 6.6). Many Japanese endorse the idea of "*En* (fate)" when it comes to relationships, of which I am not an exception. I, too, have experienced subsequent coincidental events, which led me to my current partner. My wife and I firmly believe that the god(s) of *Izumo-taisha* kindly took our case and tied the knot for us. As such, god(s) is/are in charge of creating and keeping a tie between people. This "passive" view of relationship characterizes the master narrative of matchmaking.

Figure 6.5 *Matchmaking Gods (Izumono kunino ooyashirono zu, 1862). Shimane Museum of Ancient Izumo*

Kaneko (1997) explained Japanese religious attitude through the concept of *Okage* (kindness of the deity) and *Tatari* (divine punishment).[1] In his theory, "Belief in Soul" is largely characterized by the sense of *Amae,*[2] a passive love or a need for dependency where individuals simply depend on gods to be looked after and taken care of. According to Kaneko (1997), a Japanese traditional phrase, "When in trouble, all you can do is to pray" describes the typical Japanese attitude towards conflicts and troubles in general where people passively watch the event unfold and simply wait for god(s) to intervene and remove the trouble. A *Shinto* word *Kannagara* similarly describes the virtue of ultimate passivity and unwillingness to take an action, as people let go of their control in life and trust in god(s) to lead their way. This narrative is often seen in times of natural disasters, where Japanese people seek a way to coexist with nature in harmony, refusing to stand up against difficulties that they are facing. This master narrative possibly explains some of the recent popularity of LOHAS (Lifestyles of Health and Sustainability), "ecology" as well as the "spirituality" movement in Japan.

Figure 6.6 *Match-making prayer event. Photo by Katsuya Sakai*

4. A Case Study of "Matchmaking"

To further investigate the contents of matchmaking narratives, I conducted an interview with one of the *Shinto* believers. We followed the interview protocols and procedures used in Yamada (2003) and Kawashima (2011).

The interviewee, Mrs. A is in her 50s and a member of my *shrine* (*Kousha*) along with her husband and a daughter. She previously mentioned that *En* of *Izumo-taisha* brought her and her husband together, which prompted me to ask her to be a part of the study. We could not include the entire transcript to due to space limitations, but the account described below summarizes a master narrative of matchmaking typically found in Japan.

4.1 Before Her Visit to *Izumo-Taisha*

The accounts below describe where Mrs. A was in her life before visiting *Izumo-taisha*.

S (Interviewer): *I heard that you were a teacher when you got married.*

Mrs. A: *Yes. It was my first time going on a trip by myself, and I was going to Izumo-taisha. My parents passed early on…*

S: *When you were only 29? That early?*

Mrs. A: *Yes, my father passed away when I was four due to stomach cancer, and my mother passed when I was 21 because of an autoimmune disease. I was an only child, so I became all alone.*

S: *Really, is that right.*

Mrs. A: *I have no siblings, so when I was a student, I stayed at my uncle's house. When I started working, I rented an apartment and lived alone. But then after a year or so, I moved back to his house where I used to live. My uncle was my guardian and was like my parent. I kept wondering if I would be single for the rest of my life. My aunt and guardians would try to help me by arranging for a lot of matchmaking meetings, but none of them worked out. While all of my friends got married, I didn't really go on a date or have anyone I was interested in. I turned 29, and had no idea if I could ever get married. I did have a fulfilling career, but was worried that I would end up staying single. Then I thought about* Izumo-taisha, *which is famous for matchmaking.*

Although marriage had always been in her mind, she did not have a chance to act upon that wish. It is noteworthy that she decided to go on a trip to *Izumo-taisha* with the hope for good matchmaking, so that it would possibly push herself forward for marriage.

4.2 A Change after Her Visit

The accounts below describe the change that occurred after her visit to *Izumo-taisha*.

> Mrs. A: *I was talking to my friend about my trip, and told her that I wished for good En for a future partner if it was god's will. My friend's mother overheard the conversation and said, "I didn't know you were that keen on getting married." So, a friend of my friend's mom introduced me to a person, who is now my husband. We set up a matchmaking meeting and met with each other. As we talked, I started to feel like we had a special connection, a so-called En (fate). Later when I met his mother and his relatives, we found out that my husband's mom's best friend was my great aunt. That makes me a daughter of his mom's best friend's relatives. That's when we all realized that we, in fact, do have a special connection with each other. On top of that, we also found out that my aunt, whom I used to live with, and his mom were acquaintances.*
>
> S: *How was that?*
>
> Mrs. A: *They used to go to the same girls high school. My aunt was a star volleyball player and was kind of popular among the students. My aunt didn't know about my husband's mom, but she knew my aunt. So, she was like, "Oh, are you related to Mrs. B?"*
>
> S: *When did this matchmaking meeting take place in relation to your trip to Izumo-taisha?*
>
> Mrs. A: *I went on that trip in fall, and met my husband in winter, so only three months later or so. My husband lost his father early on, too, so we both are kind of used to making decisions on our own. We fought a lot, and often had arguments because neither of us gave in to the other person. But, in the end, I came to understand that it was En that brought us together. After all, all the people who had En with us made it possible for us to meet each other. I truly feel that it was not just a coincidence, but it was people with En who brought us together.*

Mrs. A and her husband learned that they both lost their fathers at young age, which seemed to have deepened the connection between them as they shared the same sense of grief, and as a result, they developed sympathy towards each other. Her story fits the plot of "Holy Story" (Yamada, 2000) where people leave their fates to a "supernatural power" that is beyond human understanding, when they overcome grief. In particular, Yamada (2000) claimed that, "It is easier for us to feel a greater power at work that is beyond humans when we feel like we have little control over our lives (p. 103)," and that, "when good things happen, people feel like it is an invaluable gift from the dead, rather than something they earned themselves" (p. 103). Replacing the word "the dead" with "god(s)" or "a god of *Izumo-taisha*," Mrs. A's story clearly follows the religious narrative of "Holy story."

Another noteworthy characteristic of Mrs. A's narrative is that she spoke of multiple incidents and facts that she and her husband had discovered. From his mother being an acquaintance of her relatives there are many connections that they were surprised to find. Since her visit to *Izumo-taisha* occurred only a few months prior to the matchmaking meeting, Mrs. A concluded that these connections are the result of *En* that the god of *Izumo-taisha* brought, rather than "just a coincidence" or "a frequent event that happens at random."

4.3 Married Life

> S: *Do you still feel a sense of* En *sometimes even after you got married?*
>
> Mrs. A: *Quite often. It could be a book that we both read when we were single. We often say things like, "I used to like reading this book" "Really? I did, too." Or, the way we spend money. Neither of us is really known as a stingy person, so we both agree and say, "If you see something you like, just buy it." Haha. We don't even ask the price when the other person buys something. We don't have any argument about money, really. I don't even know exactly how much my husband makes or how much bonus he gets annually.*

Clearly, Mrs. A and her husband continue to find many things they share in common. Although they do have some differences, Mrs. A consistently chooses to focus on the parts they share, which she considers evidence for the *En* that god blessed them with. It seems that such positive way of thinking and particular way of narrating a story has influenced their daughter's worldview, as described below.

4.4 The Daughter's Story

> S: *Does finding things in common still happen today?*
>
> Mrs. A: *Yeah, my daughter is now 25 and has some interesting stories. She used to have a part time job during her senior year in college at this local Buddhist temple, called C Fudou-son near our house.[3] She was selling amulets during busy seasons between the end of the year and the beginning of the new year. Shortly after, she got a full-time job offer. On the first day of work, she saw an amulet from that very temple on the wall of her new office.*
>
> S: *Wow, that truly shows that there was* En.
>
> Mrs. A: *Not only that, but right around that time, I went on a trip to Shikoku Island (in western Japan) and visited D Shrine to wish for a blessing on my daughter's job hunt. There, E Construction Company was doing some repair work on some parts of the shrine. Later, we learned that the company she got a job offer from was affiliated with the E Construction Company. Who would have ever thought? My daughter thought this could be En. So we were saying, "Aren't we all so blessed by 'Kamisama (God)'s network'?" Later on, we visited the shrine and thanked the god(s). Even recently, she has encountered something like this and said, "What it all comes down to is 'Kamidanomi (Praying to god for help in times of trouble)'."*
>
> S: *I see, that's how she feels.*
>
> Mrs. A: *I think that's how most Japanese people naturally feel. Of course, you try your best, but at least we could pay a visit to a shrine and pray to god to ensure a good outcome. Ha ha.*

The interesting fact is that she is applying her "Matchmaking" narrative not only to her daughter's marriage, but also to her job-hunting experience. Oddly enough, this is rather common, as people talk about *En* as what ties a person to a job, or school, or even money. Although *En* originally refers to a tie between people, many think that it is *En* that determines one's life. In other words, the "matchmaking" narrative encompasses a passive attitude towards life where one simply tries his or her best and waits to see how life unfolds. A well-known Japanese phrase, "Do your best and leave the rest to god" stems from this line of thought, making it a humble, virtuous narrative especially when someone succeeds and does not take credit for it. The interviewee and her family gave me the impression that they tend to be optimistic in general, perhaps due to their strong belief that *Kamisama* (God)'s network will work itself out, taking care of all the details for them. This particular case seems to reflect the power of faith in *Shintoism*.

5. Conclusion

In an attempt to "psychologize" *Shintoism* and reveal the root of "the Japanese way of thinking," I have explored *Shinto* narratives that fundamentally, and often unconsciously, impact Japanese people. The examples, such as the master narratives of *Mizuninagasu*, inextricably relate to *Shinto's* ideology and seem to portray a cultural basis for *Shinto* beliefs that are so deeply embedded in Japanese culture. In order to better understand "the Japanese way of thinking," it is necessary to reconsider those beliefs that we, as Japanese, take for granted.

It is also noteworthy that in this study, we gained much insight through interviews. Although the number of subjects was limited, identifying a pattern based on the quantitative data and following up on them qualitatively seems essential in understanding how *Shintoism* is received and practiced among people.

This study is only the beginning—the beginning of a better understanding of *Shintoism* from a psychological perspective which, in turn, leads to a deeper, broader, and more comprehensive understanding of religion as a whole. It is my hope that based on the result gained in this study, we could further investigate the core of *Shintoism* that lies underneath "the Japanese way of thinking," and reach out to those interested in *Shintoism* in a sense by doing *Kotoage* (not keeping it to ourselves) so that we have a better, brighter future together in the field of psychology of religion. *Iyasaka* (I pray that this undertaking prospers)!

Notes:

[1] Kaneko conducted a survey among the believers about illness and healing and ran a factor analysis on how people reacted to the outcome that they received (seemingly) under the gods' or Buddha's influence. The "Belief in Guardianship" factor includes a sense of gratitude as well as trust that emerged when they felt protected. This belief is the basis of the concept of *Okage* (kindness of the deity). The "Belief in Soul" factor, in contrast, includes a sense of awe and fear that people have for the forgotten gods and souls who turn into demons to bring evil and disasters into our lives. This is considered to be the basis of the concept of *Tatari* (divine punishment).

[2] *Amae* is a concept developed by Japanese Psychiatrist Takeo Doi, based on personal experience with his clients. In his book "The Anatomy of Dependency," he describes *Amae* as Japanese form of love and basic needs fulfillment where one seeks for emotional dependency. For details, see Doi (1973).

[3] *Shintoism* is an inclusive religion, and many Japanese accept and practice other religions even though this particular Fudou-son was a Buddhist temple.

7.

Unfolding Religiosity in Japan:
An Exploration of the Images of Spirituality

Masaki Kobayashi, Chuo Academic Research Institute

1. Introduction

The word "spirituality" has become more prevalent in recent years. Many experts have discussed and disagreed with each other as to how to define it. Spirituality has always been associated with "religion." However, the fact that some people identify themselves as "spiritual but not religious" further complicates the issue.

Koenig (2008), one of the leading researchers in the field, claims, "There is no universal agreement on the nebulous term *spirituality*" (p. 9). He also says, "Experts are unlikely to agree on a common definition of *spirituality* in the near future" (p. 20). In his book, Koenig dedicated a whole chapter to discussing definitions of spirituality as well as religion (or religiosity). He pointed out that there are a number of medical definitions and that the concept is too ambiguous to be exclusively defined as a part of religiosity. Koenig (2008) further presents two definitions suggested by psychologists Pargament and Hufford with different theoretical views. According to Pargament's definition, spirituality relates to an inquiry into the sacred, and it is an integral function of religiosity. Hufford, on the other hand, define spirituality as a personal relationship with supernatural existence and regards religion as a communal and institutional aspect of spirituality.

Koenig suggests that the definition used by researchers needs to be separated from the ones used by medical professionals, and recommended that Hufford's definition be used for research. In addition, he claims that the definition of spirituality should indicate some sort of relationship with religion, because spirituality not only implies religious elements, but also has been historically associated with religion or supernatural existence. While supporting the general definition of religion, his definition of religion includes non-traditional, personal or private activities, as well as non-institutional form of worships. Examples include astrology, fortune telling, magic, and folktales.

A similar but more complicated discussion exists in Japan. Perhaps due to its unique cultural context, the outlook of spirituality in Japan seems particularly chaotic. Please refer to Chapter 9 (Spirituality: Exploring Its Complexity and Potentials in Psychology), as Takahashi explains this issue in depth. A similar account can also be found in his chapter in the *Overview of Religious Psychology* (Takahashi, 2011a).

In an attempt to examine how Japanese people interpret words such as religion and spirituality, our research team developed the Images of Religion Scale. The Images of Religion Scale quantifies people's general images of religion (anything related to what is considered "sacred") and enables us to visualize such images by using the 5-point Likert Scale across two dimensions: "Institutional-Personal" and "Superficial–Profound." We selected 14 items related to religion: "Religion, Prayer, Buddhism, Zazen (meditation), Consultation with a medium, Shintoism, Festivals, Christianity, Spirituality, Ascetic practices under waterfalls, Pilgrimages, Visits to power spots, Fortune-telling, and New religions." For the purpose of this study, we did not define these 14 terms and left them to participants' own interpretation.

The "institutional-personal" scale was developed partly by analyzing the ongoing discussion on the definitions of religion and spirituality. In particular, we relied heavily on Shimazono's influential and well-supported theory on this topic. In his book, *Modern Religion and Spirituality* (2012), Shimazono argues that over the years, people's views on religion have shifted away from the "system" in which religions often take form to the "personal." As a result of this, people started to perceive religion and spirituality as separate entities, the former focusing more on the "system" while the latter on the "personal" side. He claims that this trend contributed to the notion of "spiritual but not religious" people. Although Shimazono used the word "system," we decided to use "institutional religion" instead, for clearer understanding by lay people.

The second dimension, Superficial and Profound, was inspired by the discussion held among our team of researchers as several noted how spiritual matters are "lightly" received by Japanese. For example, the word "spirituality" is often featured in variety shows on TV, and countless numbers of "spiritual" books have been published without being given much thought. Moreover, spiritual conventions (supi-con) and spiritual markets (supi-ma), where dubious artifacts are demonstrated and sold, symbolize the consumption oriented and disposable images of spirituality that are currently prevalent in Japan. In some cases, however, spiritual matters are dealt with in a serious tone, reflecting the ambiguous and confusing nuances of this concept in Japan. Thus, the dimension of Superficial and Profound was added to more accurately capture the image of religion and spirituality. Figure 7.1 shows the instructions and the items on the dimension of Institutional-Personal scale.

The following items are things that are related to something 'sacred.' What institutional or personal images does each item call up in you? Please indicate what your image is by circling your choice below. You may also circle 'I don't know' or 'I don't want to answer.'

	Very institutional	Somewhat institutional	Neither	Somewhat personal	Very personal	I don't know	I don't want to answer
Religion						( )	( )
Prayer						( )	( )
Buddhism						( )	( )
Zazen (meditation)						( )	( )
Consultation with a medium						( )	( )
Shintoism						( )	( )
Festivals						( )	( )
Christianity						( )	( )
Spirituality						( )	( )
Ascetic practices under waterfalls						( )	( )
Pilgrimages						( )	( )
Visits to power spots						( )	( )
Fortune-telling						( )	( )
New religions						( )	( )

Figure 7.1 Institutional–Personal Scale

2. Composite Image of Religion among All Participants

The descriptive statistics include frequency distribution, mean, and standard deviation (n = 6,620) (see Table 7.1). In our analysis, the Institutional-Personal and Superficial-Profound dimensions were set orthogonally as the x-axis and y-axis respectively, creating quadrants: Institutional–Profound, Institutional-Superficial, Personal-Profound, and Personal–Superficial (see Figure 7.2). The 5-point Likert items correspond to -2, -1, 0, 1 and 2 on the scale. For the Institutional-Personal dimension, "Very institutional," "Somewhat institutional," "Neither institutional nor personal, "Somewhat personal," and "Very personal" were assigned -2, -1, 0, 1 and 2, respectively (Note that a negative number simply indicates a location in the quadrants and not a negative image). For the Superficial-Profound dimension, "Very superficial," "Somewhat superficial," "Neither superficial nor profound," "Somewhat profound," and "Very profound" were assigned -2, -1, 0, 1 and 2, respectively. Although we included an "I don't know" option to decrease having invalid responses and an "I don't want to answer" option to alleviate participants' stress levels, these responses were not included in this analysis.

The average for Religion was (-.99, -.98), falling in the Institutional-Profound quadrant. The average for Spirituality, on the other hand, was (.52, .03), supporting Shimazono's theory that the perception of Spirituality is generally more personal than that of Religion. Furthermore, relatively even distribution of items across all quadrants suggests the validity of the two dimensions; Shintoism, Buddhism, Religion, and Christianity in the Institutional-Profound quadrant, New religion and Festivals in the Institutional-Superficial quadrant, Ascetic practices under waterfalls, Pilgrimages, Zazen (meditation), and Prayer in the Personal-Profound quadrant, and Visits to power spots, Consultation with a medium, Fortune-telling, and Spirituality in the Personal-Superficial quadrant.

Focusing on the Institutional-Personal axes, participants rated Festival as the most institutional, while Fortune-telling as the most personal. On the Superficial-Profound axes, Visits to power spots was the most superficial and Christianity had the most profound image. This result could be due to the large number of Christian participants in this study (See appendix for the details of J-MARS project). People perceived Consultation with a medium and Visits to power spots as superficial, probably due to their strong association with the self-claimed medium figures frequently seen on variety shows on TV.

Table 7.1 Frequency Distribution, Means, and Standard Deviations for *Institutional-Personal* and *Superficial-Profound* Scores

	Institutional - Personal			Superficial - Profound		
	Mean	SD	n	Mean	SD	n
Religion	-0.99	1.18	6,238	-0.98	1.04	6,201
Prayer	0.56	1.29	6,298	-0.94	1.03	6,275
Buddhism	-0.64	1.13	5,890	-0.83	1.03	5,939
Zazen (meditation)	0.63	1.28	5,830	-0.61	1.04	5,823
Consultation with a medium	0.94	1.32	5,299	0.63	1.20	5,538
Shintoism	-0.42	1.15	4,578	-0.53	1.09	4,860
Festivals	-1.11	1.07	6,207	0.06	1.14	6,139
Christianity	-0.93	1.17	6,132	-1.01	1.02	6,090
Spirituality	0.52	1.20	3,558	0.03	1.14	3,761
Ascetic practices under waterfalls	1.18	1.08	5,857	-0.20	1.12	5,794
Pilgrimages	0.72	1.22	5,345	-0.26	1.03	5,385
Visits to power spots	1.13	1.09	5,907	0.71	1.04	5,858
Fortune-telling	1.20	1.09	6,140	0.56	1.08	6,087
New religions	-0.86	1.32	4,595	0.46	1.25	4,691

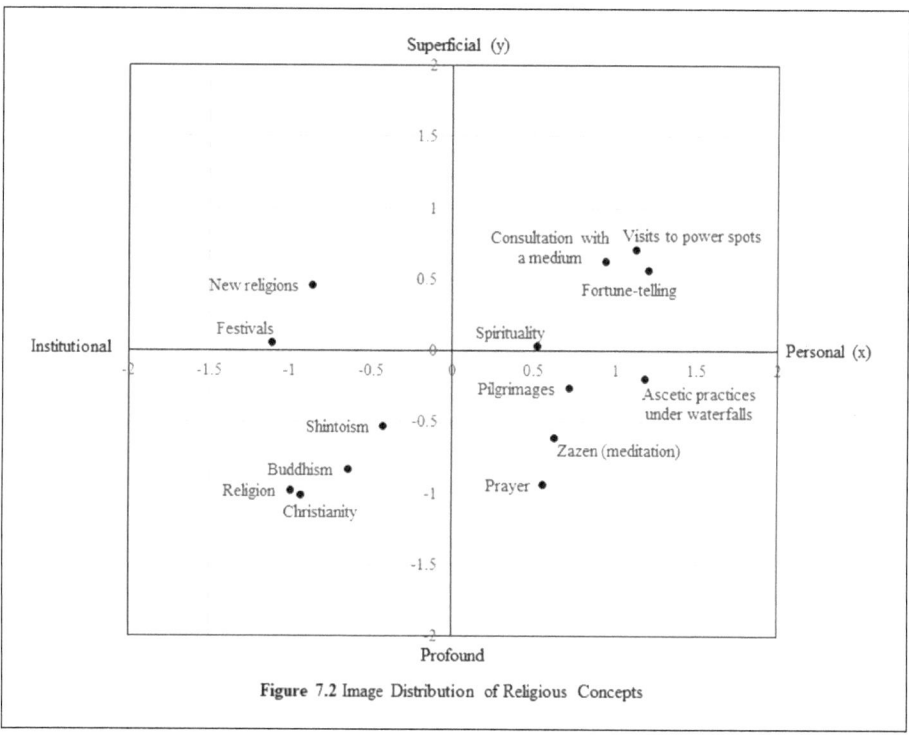

Figure 7.2 Image Distribution of Religious Concepts

3. The Image of Religion across Age Groups

First, we divided our participants into three age groups: Youth (12 to 25 years of age), Adults (26 to 64), and Older adults (65 to 93). We then visually plotted the means of Religion and Spirituality on the two dimensional Institutional-Personal and Superficial-Profound axes for each age group (See Figure 7.3; Other descriptive data are shown in the Table 7.2).

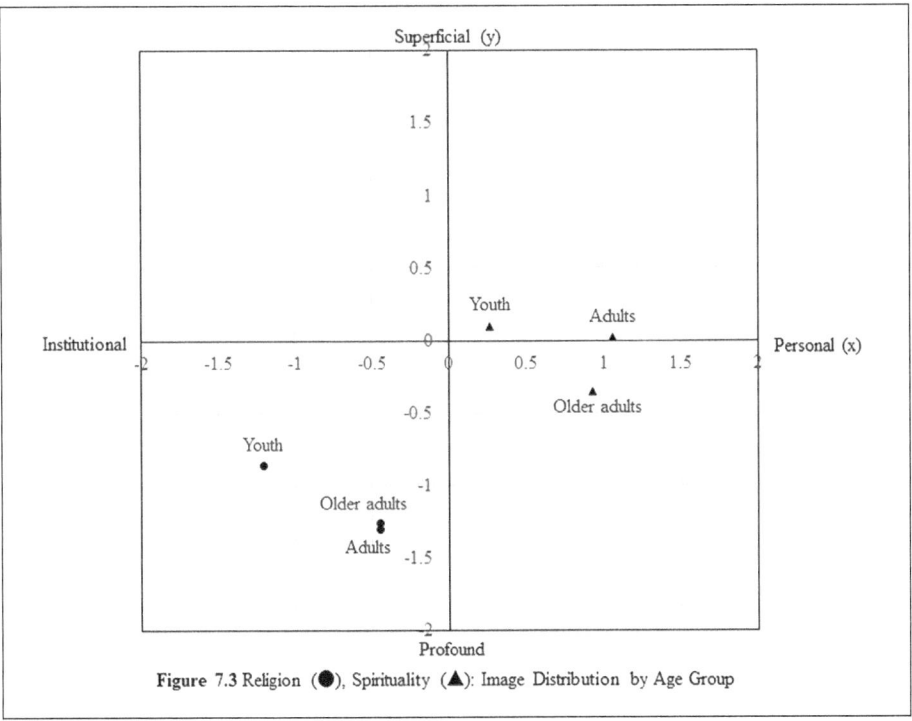

Figure 7.3 Religion (●), Spirituality (▲): Image Distribution by Age Group

Table 7.2 Means (Standard Deviation), Frequency Distribution, F Value for Religion and Spirituality across *Institutional-Personal* and *Superficial-Profound* Dimensions Across Three Groups

	Youth	Adults	Older adults	F (df)
"Religion": Institutional - Personal	-1.21 (0.98) 4,460	-0.45 (1.42) 1,013	-0.45 (1.48) 765	285.96 ** (2, 6,235)
"Religion": Superficial - Profound	-0.86 (1.05) 4,425	-1.30 (0.89) 1,013	-1.26 (0.98) 763	110.68 ** (2, 6,198)
"Spirituality": Institutional - Personal	0.27 (1.17) 2,355	1.06 (1.07) 805	0.93 (1.19) 398	170.76 ** (2, 3,555)
"Spirituality": Superficial - Profound	0.10 (1.10) 2,532	0.02 (1.17) 825	-0.35 (1.21) 404	27.79 ** (2, 3,758)
Multiple Comparison, Tukey-Method				
"Religion": Institutional - Personal	Youth < Adults, Older adults **			
"Religion": Superficial - Profound	Youth > Adults, Older adults **			
"Spirituality": Institutional - Personal	Youth < Adults, Older adults **			
"Spirituality": Superficial - Profound	Youth, Adults > Older adults **			

**$p < .01$

For Religion, the average points for all age groups fall on the lower left Institutional-Profound quadrant. The Youth had a more Institutional and Superficial image of Religion as compared to the older two groups.

With three age groups as categorical variables and average values of Institutional-Personal and Superficial-Profound scores as dependent variables, we conducted a one-way Analysis of Variance (ANOVA) for both Spirituality and Religion. For Spirituality, all groups had similar images of spirituality (either Personal-Superficial or Personal-Profound). However, Youth and Adult groups had a more Superficial image while Older Adult had a more Profound image of Spirituality. Those differences were all statistically significant ($p<.01$) (See Table 7.2).

To see which age groups are significantly different from each other, we conducted a Tukey multiple comparison test. Comparing the average points of Religion on the Institutional-Personal dimension, Youth had a significantly more Institutional image of religion than Adults and Older Adults ($p < .01$). There was no significant difference between Adult and Older adult groups (A lower score means a more Institutional image while a higher score means a more Personal image). Likewise, the average points of Religion on the Superficial–Profound dimension show that Youth perceived Religion as significantly more Superficial than Adult and Older Adult groups ($p < .01$). There was no significant difference between Adult and Older Adult groups on the Superficial-Profound dimension (A higher score means more Superficial while lower score means more Profound). In summary, the Adult and Older Adult groups had similar views on Religion, while the Youth group had more Institutional and Superficial image of Religion.

Shimazono (2012) points out that the rigid, institutional character of religion is the main reason young people have lost interest in it. Our data are clearly consistent with this assumption that our young participants perceived religion as not only Institutional but also Superficial.

In terms of Spirituality, the Youth group had a significantly more Institutional image as compared to the Adult and Older Adult samples ($p <. 01$). There was no significant difference between the Adult and Older Adult groups. For the Superficial-Profound dimension, the Older Adults perceived Spirituality as more Profound than the Youth and Adult groups ($p <. 01$) did. There was no significant difference between the latter two. In summary, the Youth group had a more Institutional and Superficial image of Spirituality than the Older Adults, and the Adult group shared a similar image of Spirituality with the Older Adult on the Institutional-Personal dimension and with the Youth on Superficial-Profound dimension. In short, while there appears to be no consistent pattern, the images of Spirituality do vary across these three age groups.

This result is consistent with Takahashi's (2011a) claim that the Japanese word "spirituality" (スピリチュアリティ) is quite new to the Japanese lexicon and that people of different cohorts may not have a consistent image of the concept. Our data seem to suggest that, for whatever the reasons, the Adult cohort is most likely to be uncertain about the image of spirituality. Takahashi speculated that these age differences in conceptualization might be partially due to either developmental changes or a cohort effect and presented the finding that the young and middle-aged adults often perceived spirituality as a more abstract, ability-based concept than the older age group who perceived it as a more concrete, experience-based concept. Although the result of the present study did not reveal the reason the scores significantly differ among age groups, it is noteworthy that both this study and that of Takahashi's support the notion of a generational gap in understanding spirituality.

4. Conclusion

This study examined how religion and spirituality were conceptualized in Japan. Based on literature review and the empirical data presented, it is safe to say that these two concepts seem to be drifting apart from each other and that different cohorts conceptualize them in unique ways. Although we could not offer a thorough analysis or explanation in this chapter due to space limitations, these findings made it clear that there is a need for further investigation on the concept of religion and spirituality from various perspectives. It is our hope that this study helps to initiate the start of such exploration.

8.

The World of Religion among Those Who Claim To Be Non-Religious

Ayumu Arakawa, Musashino Art University

An action can have multiple meanings and goals. For example, "eating" entails not only taking in nutrients but also satisfying the appetite, changing one's mood, releasing stress, satisfying curiosity, killing time, communicating with others, abusing oneself, and so forth.

Similarly, "religion" may entail the knowledge of a faith tradition as well as certain beliefs, attitudes and behaviors (what I mean by religion/faith here follows the definition in Chapter 1), and thus it is a multidimensional and not a unidimensional concept. A person is seen as a devout Buddhist if he or she regularly attends Buddhist gatherings, is active in the faith community, and is well-versed in Buddhist teachings. However, such behavior may be simply motivated by the desire to be social (e.g., having a cup of tea with friends) and/or the fear of being lonely. In contrast, other individuals may not regard themselves as religious or engage in such behaviors, yet feel some supernatural existence in daily life. I believe they are both religious in different ways.

I am certain that such diverse ideas regarding what constitutes religion have been common since antiquity; however, the behavioral models for being religious and possible personal stories of what being religious means may have been more limited in the past. As such, the distance among religious knowledge, beliefs, behaviors, and attitudes were closely intertwined in the past, and it was easier to discern the boundary between being religious and not being religious.

In recent times, various constraints and pragmatic religious rules have been loosened (the temporal factor) while the number of religions has increased. Further, as religion has become more relativistic with increasing religious tolerance and diversity (the religious relativistic factor), people no longer subscribe to a pre-packaged religious tradition but to their own set of ideas (of course, only to a certain extent). Although it is interesting to ask what the essence of religion is, I believe it is even more worthwhile to explore the types of knowledge, principles, attitudes, and behaviors that have emerged as a result of either religions (as defined as a sociocultural resource) or religious beliefs and feelings accrued during the developmental processes (something more psychological than the socio-cultural).

We do not constantly think about laws and sciences, nor do we talk to experts in those fields on a daily basis. Yet, that does not mean that we ignore them. Although we may not be aware of it, we do act based on what we know about law and science, and if necessary, we seek advice from the experts. So it is with religion. Whether we are aware of our religious conviction or follow a certain tradition, we must explore how we access the religious elements of our daily lives and how our actions are influenced by religions (unconsciously). Assessing, or even discerning, these phenomena may be challenging, however. While the meaning of our actions may have originated from religion, what we do today often no longer has religious meaning to us (e.g., simply imitating the behaviors of our parents). For example, in Japan we generally prefer to perform funeral rituals according to traditional Buddhism simply because it is customary and convenient. Even though such a preference has nothing to do with one's religious convictions, we may have easier access to that religion if we should feel the "need" for a higher power.

1. The World Views of Those Who Claim To Be Non-Religious

What about the world viewed by those who claim to be non-religious? In its extreme forms, it is easy to describe such views. According to the Quran these people are described as lost or deviated from the Way; the Bible states, "...as for those who are corrupted and do not believe, nothing is pure, in fact, both their minds and consciences are corrupted" (Titus 1:15); and Buddhism teaches that those who do not believe would be distressed and conflicted [or will suffer and find no peace in life](e.g., Dhammapada, Ch.7). Those who are religious may see those without faith as, "people who cannot be saved," and think that even though there is/are god(s)/Buddha who provide(s) pure pleasure, those who have no faith would never even notice this fact and simply regard everything as random events. In short, the believer may think that the view of "anything goes" is extremely shallow.

It is surprising, however, that those who are non-religious claim that their views (of this world at least) are not at all shallower in comparison to those who are religious. For example, regardless of their religious conviction, 73.2% of Japanese disagree with the statement, "Human life has no purpose" (ranked first among 40 countries surveyed) (ISSP Research Group, 2012). In other words, the majority of those who claim to have no religious faith believe that they have a purpose in life and are doing quite well. Is this because they "don't know the true purpose and are being misled," as the non-religious claim, or is the notion of the "true purpose of existence" just an idea imposed by the faithful? From the perspective of the believers, they feel that they do not share the same "language" with non-believers and that people without faith simply have to wait for a moment in life when they will encounter a situation that requires faith.

2. Japanese Who Claim To Be Non-Religious

According to the ISSP Research Group (2012), 62% of the Japanese, the lowest among 40 participating countries, responded negatively to the question, "Are you affiliated with any religion? (It must be noted that China, generally perceived as the least religious country, was not included in this study). The low rate of religious affiliation in Japan is nothing new. In fact, it has been very consistent since the end of WWII.

While only 32.2% claim that they have a religious faith, 65.4% of those survey said that they are either "sure" or "almost sure" that there are god(s)/Buddha (Manabe, 2010). This is not atypical, and a similar pattern is seen in Hong Kong, Korea, and Taiwan (Hayashi, 2010). Further, there appears to be an increase in behaviors that are rooted in religious faith, while the rate of religious affiliation remains low. For example, the rate of non-religious people who believe in the after-world increased from 20% in 1958 to 38% in 2008 (Hayashi, 2010). In another report (e.g., NHK, 2019), the number of people who visit graveyards and believe in fortune telling has increased since the 1970s. Similarly, Hayashi (2012) found an increasing number of people who "feel calm and serene in front of religious altars," "feel the presence of spirits in the mountains, rivers, grass, and trees," and "feel the need to make a thanksgiving offering for worn out tools such as sewing needles." Similarly, according to the data from the ISSP (2012), among non-religious people, Japanese ranked second highest (55.8%), following South Africans (65.9%), in the number of people who "believe in ancestral supernatural powers affecting the living" (followed by Taiwan, the distant third with 36.1%). In short, contrary to our general expectation, there seems to be an increase in folk beliefs rooted in religion, and quite a substantial number of Japanese who identify as non-religious engage in some type of religious behavior.

The data from the J-MARS project also yielded similar results. Figure 8.1 summarizes religious beliefs and relevance of religions among religious college students (Matsushima & Arakawa, 2015). The results reveal that a) a large portion of the religious students felt that religion was unnecessary; and b) even among non-religious students some felt that religion was necessary.

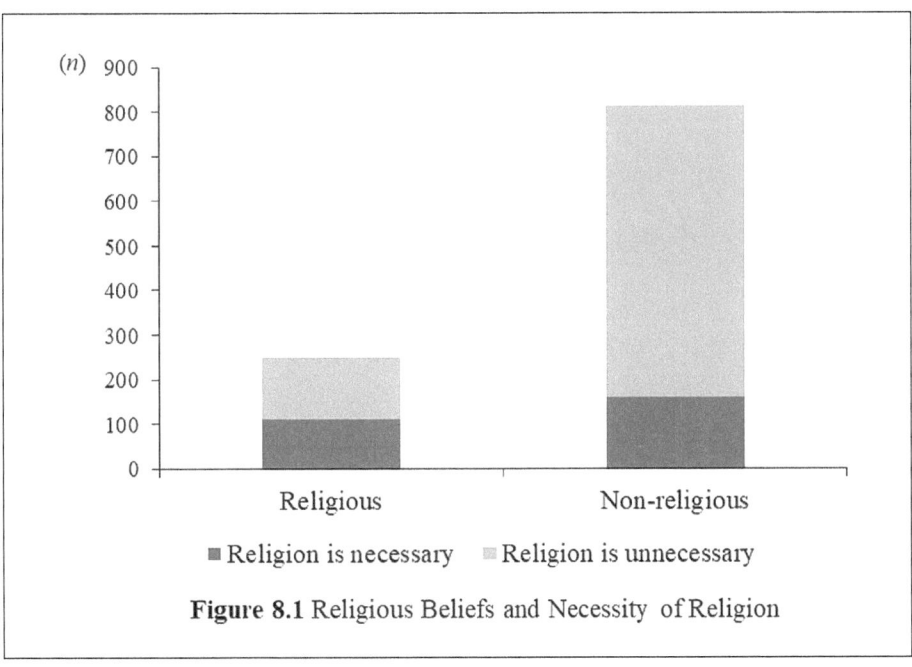

Figure 8.1 Religious Beliefs and Necessity of Religion

These "religious" behaviors and attitudes are likely to be rooted in what Kaneko (1999) defines as *okage* and *tatari*. Further, Manabe (2010) found from his cross-cultural analyses that while "religious behaviors" (e.g., reading the Bible or other scriptures, going to church or attending mass, etc.) are common in Germany, Japanese tend to engage in "traditional or customary practices" (e.g., visiting cemetery and praying at altars) and "event-related behavior" (e.g., buying amulets and visiting shrines). The latter two behaviors originated in religion(s) but became secular customs at some point. In other words, the individuals who engage in these types of behavior do not have faith or a sense of belonging to any specific religious groups. As was stated at the beginning of this chapter, the behavior still can be regarded as religious; however, these individuals cannot rely on the support system offered by a religious organization, neither do they abide by the established rules within any religious organization, nor do they avail themselves of the opportunity found in many religious traditions of going through processes concerning the self and important life events with the help of religious leaders and fellow believers (Figure 8.2). In the next section, I will explore two systems (meaning making and unconscious elements) related to different forms of religion.

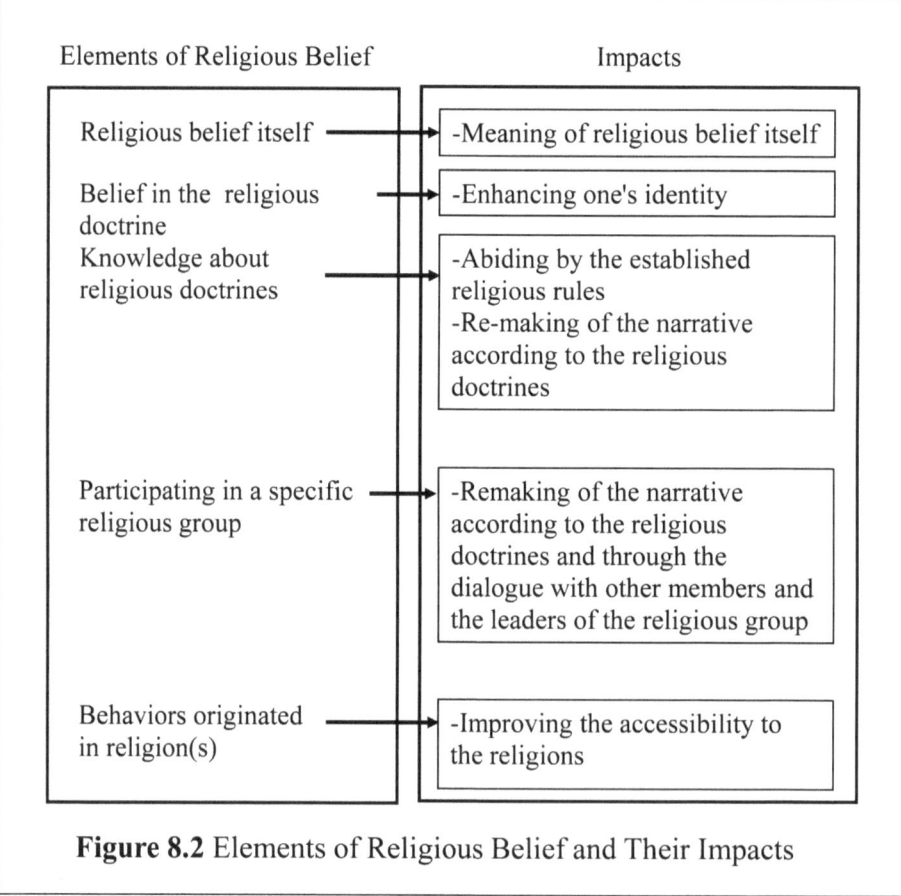

Figure 8.2 Elements of Religious Belief and Their Impacts

3. What is the Function of Meaning Making Systems within Faith?

Religious faith functions as a meaning-making system that defines the world and all that takes place. This system defines who we are and helps us comprehend, navigate, and organize these events (Park, 2014). There are other meaning-making systems, such as those based on science and natural laws, but the religious meaning-making system has two powerful devices that these other systems lack. First, while the other two systems provide explanations, interpretations, predictions and control by guiding individuals either to accept knowledge (in the scientific system with logic) or the phenomena (according to natural law), the religious meaning-making systems have "a truth seeking device" [1] which provides interpretations that are beyond human perception and comprehension (e.g., via-conversation with god(s)).[2]

Second, a religious system also provides an inclusive meaning making function. Other systems, such as those based on science and natural laws, cannot answer the questions like, "Why do I exist?" "Why do I, but not others, have to suffer?" "Why do I have to continue to live?" Also, only a religious system can answer the question often posed by children, such as, "Where do we go after we die?" and "How come I have but other kids don't?" Hood, Hill, and Williamson (2005) argue that a religious system is more inclusive than other systems because of its "comprehensiveness" (it provides a framework for understanding and predicting phenomena), "accessibility" (with more opportunities to meet/encounter) and "transcendence" (accepting the existence of higher being(s)) while also providing a "direct claim" about cause and effect (explicit existential answers). This is probably the reason why people "need" religion (or at least acknowledge the need for religion) especially in times of crisis.

It is interesting to note that even those who appear to use "a truth seeking device" often claim that they are non-religious. For example, Arakawa and Matsushima (2016) found that regardless of whether they have a religious affiliation or not, young people believed that science was "less likely" to offer truth about the universe ($n=82$). This finding suggests that people in general tend to believe in the existence of the truth that is beyond our scientific knowledge.

Although people yearn for the truth, which they see as something beyond our scientific knowledge, why do they not seek that answer in religion or accept that their belief is religious in nature? To answer these questions, I will explore what "being religious" means.

4. What Does "Being Religious" Mean?

Rambo (1993) points out four necessary systems for understanding religious conversion. First, during a religious conversion, one's epistemological frameworks and culture often interfere with religion. Second, the social status of religious organizations and the role of non-religious systems may influence access to those religious organizations. Third, how a person makes sense of personal experiences, including hardships, has a huge impact on the process of conversion. Fourth, one must go through not only psychological changes but also religious experiences and feelings during a conversion. In order to understand the religiosity of non-religious Japanese, cultural and social systems must be highlighted. Especially, we must pay a close attention to the micro (e.g., family, friends, communities, etc.) and the macro (e.g., social attitudes toward various religions) and the contexts of the social system regarding religious conversion.

In effect, the macro context regarding religion is very negative in Japan. For example, Arakawa and Matsushima (2016) found that both religious and non-religious university students liked people with scientific minds more than those with unscientific minds, while non-religious students liked religious people less than non-religious people. By the same token, the ISSP data (2012) also revealed that compared to the average (3.8%) of all nations involved, 57.0% of the Japanese surveyed disagreed with the statement, "We must respect all religions." These findings clearly suggest that non-religious Japanese feel quite negative toward being religious.

One approach to understanding how negative attitudes toward religion would influence someone's unwillingness to be religious is to study the process of creating personal narratives regarding religions. According to the three-layer model of genesis (Sato, 2009), changes in the self-narrative occur through daily experiences in micro-, meso-, and macro-levels (see Figure 8.3). For example, various events in daily life may have created a self-narrative of "God of the established religion does not exist" at micro-level, which may or may not be consistent with his/her self-narrative at the macro-level. When inconsistencies occur frequently and/or in a profound way, one may interpret (at the meso-level) an ordinary event (at micro-level) as a "sign." If that interpretation is a part of a larger narrative of a given religious discipline, he/she may contact a religious organization. If the person then feels a fit between his/her experience and the interpretation provided by that religion, then a religious conversion follows at macro-level. Once the self-narrative is altered, it is difficult to see/experience things in a way consistent with the non-religious narrative. This process is similar to the visual perception of figure and ground. Once a person sees a figure, it is difficult to see the figure as a ground.[3]

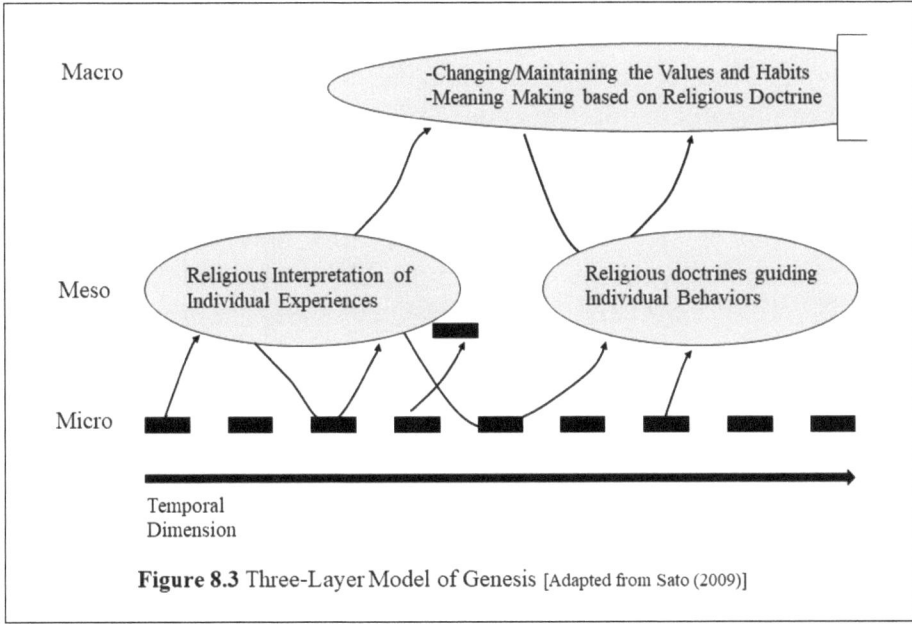

Figure 8.3 Three-Layer Model of Genesis [Adapted from Sato (2009)]

The fact that the Japanese society has a negative attitude toward religious people and organizations creates a macro-level context in which people are generally reluctant to accept a religious narrative. Instead, each individual, often via internet search, creates at the meso-level a unique, religious-like narrative that is not necessarily a part of any established religion. This tendency is expressed in the datum that 32.2% of the Japanese agree with the statement, "I am usually doubtful about the existence of god, but I still believe in some higher power's existence" (ISSP Research Group, 2012). This type of religious view that accepts higher powers (e.g., panpsychism, animism) in the broadest sense may have a similar conceptual root as that of religious naturalism (Nishiwaki, 2004) or of those who claim to be "spiritual but not religious" in the U.S. (Wuthnow, 2007). In the case of religious naturalism, people generally accept the core discipline of *Shintoism*, but they deny that they are *Shintoists*.

On the other hand, the idea of "god(s)" without religious implications is prevalent in contemporary Japan. For example, the lyrics of popular songs often contains the word "god(s)," suggesting such a concept outside the context of established religions is "available" at both macro- and micro-levels.

5. Psychological Development of Religiosity

It is generally thought that religious beliefs and interpretations are "handed down" by something external (e.g., religious doctrine); however, they may develop internally. For example, Atran and Norenzayan (2004) argue that humans acquired a tendency to extract an "agent" responsible for external phenomena during the evolutionary process. Further, in order to reduce fear when facing one's death, an individual tends to believe in the afterworld (direct immortal concept) or hope that others would remember him or her in the future (indirect immortal concept) (Wakimoto, 2012). Similarly, Saijo (2002) argues that people pay more attention to natural phenomena, such as weather and nature, when facing death. These ideas are consistent across monotheistic and nature-based religions.

6. Making Sense of Hardships

When facing hardship, people realize that some things are beyond their control. It is then that they long for a transcendental narrative which may be religious and give meaning to the situation (e.g., "illness narrative" (Frank, 1995); "loss narrative" in spiritual care (Yamada, 2007)). This is one of the reasons why poverty, conflict, and illness are believed to trigger religious conversions. In fact, there are many people who reported that "Religion changed my perspective" during recovery after hardship (e.g., Ikeuchi & Fujiwara, 2009). On the other hand, significantly more Japanese (15.3%) than people from other countries (2.2% on average) believe that religion is useless for "Reducing hardships and sadness" (ISSP Research Group, 2012). This finding suggests that religions play only a limited role in Japan, even in the minds of those who are experiencing hardships.

7. Unconscious Elements in Religion

Even though a person does not use religiosity as a meaning making tool, this does not make that person non-religious. Here I refer to the aforementioned "unconscious elements in religion." A well-known study by Shariff and Norezayan (2007) showed that people who were primed with such words as "god" and "morality" tend to behave more altruistically than those who were not. While this study failed to be replicated in Japan (Miyatake & Higuchi, 2005), Arakawa and Matsushima (2016) found that people were more comfortable when disposing of amulets/charms or taking part in a cremation when this was done following traditional rituals than when it was done without them (Figure 8.4). This finding indicates that while people in Japan may not be aware of it, their tendency to interpret ordinary events in a religious sense is already ingrained in their culture

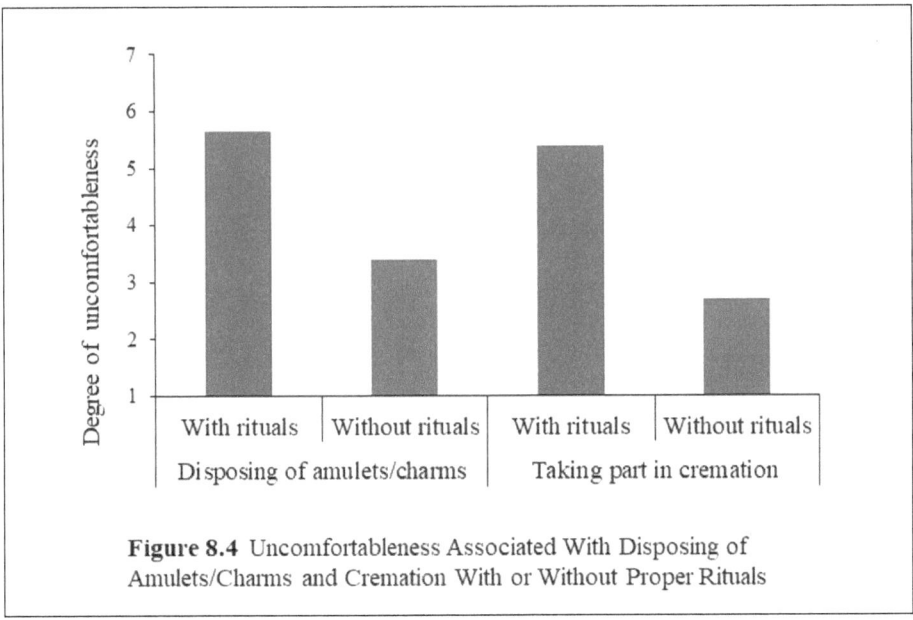

Figure 8.4 Uncomfortableness Associated With Disposing of Amulets/Charms and Cremation With or Without Proper Rituals

8. Potential for Daily Religious Behavior and Religious Interpretation Systems

There are a variety of daily behaviors that originated in faith traditions that non-Japanese people see as religious, yet people in Japan may not recognize these behavior as religious (e.g., celebrating Christmas, buying amulets, etc.). These "established behaviors" are consistent with related religious practices that may facilitate access to existing religions when necessary. In other words, this type of behavior can be understood as an entry point to various religions as the behavior shares both cultural and religious characteristics. There are plenty of examples in which religion is "utilized" in a context that is not religious at all. Memorial services performed for non-religious items illustrate this point, including scrapped personal computers (the *Bansho* temple), eyeglasses (the *Daihi-in* temple), credit cards (the *Ichihime* shrine), dentures (the *Nittai-ji* temple), and ballet slippers (*Takahoko* shrine).

9. Summary

Although a large majority of Japanese report that they are not religious, what they say may not be what they are. Many people may not engage themselves in traditional religious behavior nor realize that their behaviors are religious in nature. Yet, these people may indeed be religious because they are influenced by religious beliefs (often unconsciously) and use religion as a meaning-making framework in everyday settings. In other words, "being religious" is not a static but a dynamic process influenced by numerous elements including culture, history, and tradition among others.

Notes:

[1] The idea of a "truth seeking device" was suggested by Ms. Megumi Inamura at Musashino Art University.

[2] This explanation by religious researchers is backwards, in a sense, as they claim, that religions provide explanations to the believers. In contrast, from the perspective of a religious person, one believes in God not because this can provide explanations but because God exists.

[3] Losing one's faith is a similar process in reverse. As the inconsistencies between what a person experiences and the religious teaching increases, he/she could eventually lose faith.

9.

Spirituality: Exploring Its Complexity and Potentials in Psychology

Masami Takahashi, Northeastern Illinois University

1. Introduction

While the psychology of religion is gaining an unprecedented popularity among social scientists, the concept of spirituality is still set aside and is generally discussed only in the theological or metaphysical arenas. In this chapter, I will review my own research on spirituality from a psychological perspective while addressing its complexity and potentials in empirical science. I will also examine its historical roots followed by an overview of cross-cultural studies of the past few decades. The data and analyses of spirituality in the J-MARS project will then be presented and discussed.

2. The Complexity of Spirituality

Spirituality is regarded as one of the tricky concepts in science for at least two reasons. First, it is closely associated with religion, a domain that is generally viewed as antithetical to science. Their "rivalry" may have a beginning in the modern scientific era that includes the debate over heliocentrism vs. geocentrism in the 16th century and Descartes's claim in *Treatise of Man* that the pineal gland is the intersection of body and soul; the most recent controversy about the theory of evolution and intelligent design is still new to many of us.

Another reason that spirituality is difficult to deal with is specific to

Japan; it is an "imported" (i.e., English) word. In our recent study (Takahashi, 2011b), young Japanese people reported that they have frequently heard the term "spiritual" (phonetically spelled "*supirichuaru*" スピリチュアル) in popular media and thought that they knew what it meant. However, the participants also claimed that they have never heard of its noun form, "spirituality" ("*supirichuariti*" スピリチュアリティ), and had no idea of its meaning. In their minds these two terms are completely different words/concepts and what they know about its adjective form is exclusive to how the pop culture defines it (I will discuss later more about how the Japanese pop culture defines spirituality).

What is this somewhat familiar yet tricky concept? I will discuss why it is difficult to study spirituality as a scientific construct and analyze its socio-historical aspect, particularly its affiliation with religiosity and its uniqueness as an imported concept. I will lay out its conceptual foundation in an inclusive manner by examining where this concept came from in our history and how it is being understood across cultures including contemporary Japan. Finally, based on the data from J-MARS, I will propose how this concept should be treated (especially in Japan) in the future in the field of science.

3. Spirituality and Science

The English word "spirituality" is derived from *spiritus*, a Latin word that later became incorporated into Middle French and eventually into the English lexicon during the Middle Ages. *Spirit* was understood as a non-physical aspect, such as breath, strength, and soul, of all living things including humans. In the Judeo-Christian tradition, spirit is particularly important for it means the "breath" (of God) that gave Adam life in *Genesis*. In the West, then, with a long history and common usage of spirit, spirituality, and spiritual, it is not surprising that people are generally familiar with these concepts.

In Western psychology, the concept has over a century of history that may be traced back to William James, one of the founders of psychology (Figure 9.1). Influenced by E. Swedenborg, a scientist and a theologian, James highlighted an important role that spirit/soul played in our lives. In *The Varieties of Religious Experience* (1902), he proposed four characteristics associated with mystical or spiritual experiences that one may go through: Ineffability—direct experience that may not be expressed in words, a concept similar to *furyu monji* in *Zen* Buddhism; noetic quality—an ability to discern the essence of things; transiency—belief that mystic or spiritual experiences are short-lived; and passivity—surrendering oneself to a higher power. It is interesting to note that in his writing James maintained a scientific narrative of these experiences and did not focus on a particular religion or a religious doctrine. Perhaps, this separation of religion and science is the reason why the book is still highly regarded as a classic in psychology.

Figure 9.1 *William James. Houghton Library, Harvard University*

During the 1930s, spirituality was also held as a core construct in parapsychology. However, it coincided with the emergence of behaviorism in psychology whose focus was solely on observable behaviors. As behaviorism tried to establish itself as a (natural) scientific discipline, behaviorists vigorously rejected anything that was even remotely metaphysical and religious. This period, often referred to as the era of "psychology without psyche," came to an end when the Cognitive Revolution of the mid-20th century put forth a new paradigm in which psychology should value not only observables but also interpretations of observed human behavior. Accordingly, we now witness the revival of forbidden concepts that were once seen as unscientific, metaphysical, and religious. This revival probably inspired the idea that religion and spirituality should be studied by scientists and contributed to the movement that incorporated the American Catholic Psychological Association (later renamed as the Predivisional Psychologists Interested in Religious Issues) into Division 36 of the American Psychological Association (APA) in 1976. The APA Division 36 was again renamed, Psychology of Religion in 1993 and eventually, the Society for the Psychology of Religion and Spirituality which now plays a valuable role in leading the field including the publication of the most highly influential journal, *Psychology of Religion and Spirituality* (Reuder, 1999).

As an interest in spirituality increased in the field of psychology, Ribaudo and Takahashi (2009) examined temporal trends in spirituality research by reviewing the abstracts of all peer-reviewed articles ($N = 1,759$) listed in two large databases, *PsychInfo* and *AgeLine*, that contained "spirituality" as a key word. It was found that the number of publications increased 15-fold since 1980s to 210 per year in 2000s and that the trend is continuing. Ribaudo and Takahashi also analyzed each abstract and yielded seven distinctive research themes: Conceptual Analysis (24.1%), Measurement (20.9%), Spirituality Education (16.5%), Spiritual Intervention (21.5%), Discussion of Community Projects (4.7%), Review Articles (9.3%), and others (3.0%).

Further analyses also revealed that a recurring pattern of research contents of spirituality focusing on either theory construction (i.e., introduction of new theories and methodologies) or its application (i.e., educational programs and community interventions) exists. For instance, when spirituality research became popular in the 1980s, the research focus was mainly on theory construction, but more applied research was then reported during the late 80s and early 90s. This pattern has repeated itself several times during the past three decades. This finding suggests that spirituality is a highly complex and fluid concept influenced by the zeitgeist of the field, and thus theoretical discussions followed by more empirical research using newer definitions of spirituality recur.

4. Spirituality in Japan

Unlike the popularity of spirituality studies in the West since the 80s, the research on spirituality in Japan had been quite dormant for a long time. The concept was occasionally mentioned as *rei-sei* (霊性) or *bushou* (仏性) in the medical field, but it remained an unfamiliar concept for lay people. In fact, Takahashi et al. (2004) examined the number of publications published prior to 2003 in major databases in Japan (i.e., Medical Central Journals, National Library NDL-OPAC, and Social Gerontology DIAL) and found only 74 papers with "spirituality" (スピリチュアリティ) and 217 papers with "spiritual" (スピリチュアル) as key words. While this number has been increasing since 2003, these articles are primarily in clinical settings, particularly in end of life care at Christian hospitals, and there is clearly a lack of its discussion theoretically.

5. Spirituality and Religion

One caveat about studying spirituality is its ambiguous relationship with the concept of religiosity throughout the years. For example, the aforementioned research (Ribaudo and Takahashi, 2009; Takahashi et al., 2004) that reviewed empirical studies on spirituality found that only a handful of studies delineated the difference between the two (it was extremely rare in the Japanese literature). This lack of a clear conceptual demarcation is reflective of how our earlier predecessors treated these two concepts. Even those who distanced themselves from organized Christianity (e.g., Thomas Paine, Ben Franklin) as well as Universalists and Free Masons had a tendency not to make a clear distinction between religion and spirituality. This trend continued with certain branches of metaphysics that tried to integrate theology and science (e.g., Swedenborgianism) to the contemporary New Age movement that incorporated Yoga and Eastern meditation into spirituality.

In psychology, W. James, E. Fromm, and G. Alport, among others, recognized religiosity as an important psychological construct but never clearly distinguished it from spirituality. Ando (2006) also makes a similar point that these two concepts were rarely distinguished in psychology (especially in the clinical literature). For example, Ando claims that in the Jungian literature translated into Japanese, only religion, but not spirituality, is mentioned whereas in the transpersonal field the opposite is true; there are many references to spirituality but not to religion. While this trend is mainly due to the historical and theoretical underpinnings of each discipline, Zimbauer and Pargament (2005) suggest that people generally regard spirituality as functional, dynamic, and personal while they see religiosity as substantive, static, and institutional in a rigid dualistic framework, and that this polarization has brought more problems and confusion than clarity to the field.

In recent years, however, at least in the U.S., people are becoming more aware of the distinction. In fact, an increasing proportion of the U.S. adult population claim that they are "spiritual but not religious." This trend is especially prevalent among those who have higher educational and socioeconomic status. In addition, several influential organizations and academic journals recently began to rename themselves by including both "religion" and "spirituality" to their titles (e.g., the APA Division 36).

Nevertheless, unclarity as to where to draw a line between these two concepts in psychology still persists, and spirituality is often used as a mere synonym for religion. This confusion may reflect the fact that the U.S. is the current leader of empirical research in psychology and religion, yet it is the largest religious country in the world where over 80 % of the population identify with a particular religion. Moreover, the majority of these people believe in the story of *Genesis* over the scientific theory of evolution. In other words, a concept of spirituality that has both scientific and theological meanings is still recognized as enigmatic and difficult to deal with among many people including social scientists (Takahashi, 2011).

6. Psychological Studies of Spirituality
6.1 Our Research

As seen in the previous section, although it is not easy to define spirituality in a field of empirical study, an increasing number of psychologists have been investigating it as a scientific concept. For example, Elkins, Hedstrom, Hughes, Leaf, and Saunders (1988) analyzed humanistic psychological literature, such as the work of Jung and Frankl, and extracted nine core dimensions of spirituality: transcendence, meaning and purpose in life, mission in life, sacredness of life, material values, altruism, idealism, awareness of the tragic, and the fruits of spirituality. They then asked those who were recommended as being very spiritual in various religious organizations to evaluate these dimensions. The results revealed that these "spiritual" individuals in fact agreed that these core dimensions are important factors in their respective religions.

Similarly, in a study with a group of middle-aged ($n = 29$, mean age = 43.0, $SD=8.7$) and older ($n = 21$, mean age = 74.4, $SD=9.0$) American men and women of various religious, ethnic, and educational backgrounds, the participants were asked to define spirituality in their own words, generate a list of related descriptors, and name spiritual people they knew (Takahashi et al., 2000). The qualitative data were analyzed by two independent, trained raters: an atheist and a devout Christian. It was found that the participants perceived negative life events as turning points of their spiritual lives and that the degree to which a person is involved in religion influenced how he/she defined spirituality. It was also found that the older participants tended to use religion-related words (e.g., church, the Bible, etc.) when describing spirituality, while they were less likely than the middle-aged counterparts to name religious figures (e.g., priests, rabbi, etc.) as spiritual people they knew. In other words, for older people in this study, religion is a necessary but not sufficient condition to describe spirituality or a spiritual person.

Furthermore, the study also revealed five themes associated with spirituality regardless of one's background: religious virtues, intrapersonal strength, altruistic character, existential meaning, and transcendence (Table 9.1). While this finding is consistent with that of Elkins et al. (1988) and other studies that state spirituality is not a unidimensional but a multidimensional construct, it also revealed the need for further systematic research that would explore the meanings of spirituality and the relationships of its multiple dimensions.

Table 9.1 Five Themes Associated With Spirituality

		Example answers: "Spirituality is..."
1	Religious virtues	"It means having strong faith to God."
2	Intrapersonal strength	"It means living with faith."
3	Altruistic character	"It means caring others."
4	Existential meaning	"It means having meaning in life."
5	Transcendence	"It means realizing afterlife or other worlds."

(Takahashi et al., 2000)

Subsequently, Takahashi and Ide (2003) carried out a series of investigations on how people defined spirituality. First, we examined the semantic relations between spirituality and related key words including the five themes generated in the previous study (religious, caring, having meaning in life, transcendental, having faith, suffered hardships, wise, and intelligent). When we started this project in 2001, the phonetic translation of the English word "spiritual" (スピリチュアル) was not yet well-known (none of the older people in a pilot study recognized the word). Thus, we listed *seishin-sei* (精神性) and *rei-sei* (霊性) side by side as the translation of spirituality in these studies. The former was the most common translation of spirituality in several dictionaries whereas the latter was a commonly used translation in clinical literatures. While the study originally involved only three generations of Japanese sample including students/young (18-23 years old), their parents/middle-aged (46-58 years old), and their grandparents/older adults (67-89 years old) (total $n = 154$), we soon expanded the project to include three generations of American counterparts ($n = 219$). Furthermore, in order to shed a light on the developmental trajectory of one's spirituality, we also asked the participants to rate their own spirituality in the past, present, and future.

Several cultural and age differences were identified. First, we found significant cultural differences in the interpretation of spirituality among the age groups. For the Japanese sample, the younger and middle-aged participants thought of spirituality as an abstract concept denoting one's personal strength (i.e., having meaning in life and transcendence), whereas the older adults associated spirituality with more concrete concepts such as caring and suffered hardship. This result is consistent with previous findings that with development older people tend to understand abstract, complex concepts based on their own conceptual framework shaped by a lifetime of experience.

Second, it was also found that the older Japanese had the largest semantic distance between spiritual and religious. There are several possible reasons for this finding including the claim that the older adults tend to have an advanced cognitive faculty and are generally better able to delineate related concepts than are the younger cohorts (Baltes, 1993). Another possible explanation is that the oldest group in this study was the "pre-war cohort" (*showa hitoketa*) who grew up during the time when Japanese spiritualism was often abused by the imperial government propaganda (e.g. "the spirit of suicide missions," "the spirit of nativist Japanese") which, in turn, may have influenced them to be more sensitive in distinguishing spiritual and religious.

In contrast to these findings in the Japanese groups, it is interesting to note that the understanding of spirituality was pretty much the same for all three generations in the U.S. This is primarily due to the fact that spirituality is already imbedded as a part of everyday English lexicon and is generally understood within a well-defined frame of reference. It was also revealed that among Americans, spirituality was closely associated with having faith, religious, and caring, indicating the importance of religious and humanistic dimensions.

With regard to how people perceive their own spirituality of the past, present, and future, several cultural and generational differences were also found. For the generational difference, regardless of their cultural background, older participants evaluated themselves as more spiritual and religious than did the younger generations, suggesting a contribution of their accumulated experiences to the formation of their religious and spiritual self. That is, the longer one lives, he or she is likely to have more opportunities to contemplate existential questions, and those experiences create a foundation of one's spirituality and religious beliefs.

For the cultural differences, the American participants were significantly more likely than the Japanese to think of themselves as spiritual and religious and wished to become even more so in the future, indicating much more positive nuances of these concepts in the U.S. than in Japan. This is an indication that a "positive" concept in one culture may not necessarily carry the same valence in different cultural contexts because of different historical and cultural values associated with that concept.

In addition, we also examined an applied use of the concept of spirituality in everyday life by asking these participants to evaluate the level of spirituality of well-known individuals whose names had been pre-generated by a group of volunteers as either spiritual (Nelson Mandela, Mother Terresa, Mahatma Gandhi, and John Paul II) or not-so-spiritual (Shoko Asahara, Adolf Hitler, Bill Clinton, Saddam Hussein) (Ide & Takahashi, 2002).[1] After making sure that the participants recognized these individuals, we asked them how spiritual they thought these well-known individuals were (due to a lack of recognition by either the Japanese or American participants, we excluded Shoko Asahara and Nelson Mandela from the subsequent analyses). The results showed that the Japanese sample evaluated Hitler and Hussein as significantly more spiritual than did the American sample[2] (see Table 9.2). That is, while spirituality in the U.S. is generally regarded as an "absolute virtue" as represented by figures like Mother Terresa, the Japanese may not always perceive the concept in a positive light. This finding is indicative of the fact that the American participants emphasize the humanistic aspect of spirituality (e.g., caring and altruistic) while the Japanese, especially the young and middle-aged, saw the intrapersonal strength (e.g., transcendental) as a valuable component of spirituality. In this case, it is possible that the Japanese people might have thought the extraordinary political and military skills in Hitler and Saddam Hussein as a part of spirituality.

Table 9.2 Means (Standard Deviation) of Response to the Following Questions: "Are These People Spiritual?" and "Are These People Religious?" (5-Point Scale)

	Japanese ($n = 154$)			American ($n = 219$)		
	D/K	Religious	Spirituality	D/K	Religious	Spirituality
Hitler	14	2.61 (1.32)	2.72 (1.28)	8	1.62 (1.07)	1.52 (0.86)
Hussein	29	3.23 (1.40)	2.77 (1.37)	17	2.87 (1.37)	2.35 (1.33)

Note. D/K = "I don't know"

Nevertheless, while it is clear from these findings that the understanding of the concept is markedly different between the two groups, the limitation of this study was that there was no equivalent word for the concept of spirituality and that we had to use *seishin-sei* (精神性 or "spirit-feeling") and *rei-sei* (霊性 or "divinity-feeling") which have their own nuances tied to certain histo-cultural values.

By the mid 2000s, the phonetic translation of spirituality (スピリチュアリティ or Japanese spirituality hereafter) became well-known to the public because of the New Age "spiritual boom" in Japanese pop culture, but its usage, especially its conceptual distinction with religiosity, was unclear and confusing at best. As a result, its meaning in English and the Japanese spirituality diverged considerably from each other. Today, Japanese spirituality implies more of a concept of the occult (e.g., spirit of a previous life, paranormal phenomena, etc.) than the concept originally derived from *spiritus* or *seishin-sei* (精神性) and *rei-sei* (霊性). Even the Japanese Society for the Study of Psychology of Religion, an entity that carried out the J-MARS project and the only organization in Japan to study religion and spirituality from a psychological perspective, never adopted the word スピリチュアリティ in its official title as it may attach a "shady" nuance to the organization.

6.2 Psychological Studies of Spirituality in Japan: A Large-Scale Survey Research by J-MARS

As a part of the J-MARS project, we conducted a survey research project examining the concept of spirituality between 2012-2014 (See Appendix for a description of the project). The first step we had to take in order to carry out a large-scale psychological study of spirituality was to understand how Japanese in general perceive the popularized concept of Japanese spirituality. Gushiken (2009), one of our research members, reviewed over 300 Japanese non-academic books about Japanese spirituality in the genres such as self-help, personal development, introductory religions, para-normal, occultism, etc. and extracted the most frequently referenced themes. He then created the Japanese Spirituality Index (JSI) with six dimensions: Meaning of life, Retribution, Incarnation of psychological images, Karma, Divine protection, and Eternal soul. It is interesting to note that most of these themes are consistent with Buddhist teachings because the contents of these popular books were not so much about Western spiritual teachings or the imperial spiritualism once popular in Japan. In other words, however secular the Japanese people may be according to the available statistical data, the everyday lives of these people, including the authors and the readers of these books, are still intertwined to a great extent with traditional Buddhist ideologies and practices.

In the J-MARS project, Gushiken et al. (2013) focused on three JSI themes that had strong correlations with psychological health. Meaning of life was defined as "Things we face in life happening not randomly but with a meaning and necessity (not random and inevitable)," and represented this with five questions such as, "Things that happen in your life and people you meet are intertwined with an invisible fate (en) which helps you learn and mature. They do not happen randomly." Karma was defined as "one's behavior, either good or bad, which has consequences that will eventually come back to that person." It had four questions (e.g., "What goes around comes around. Kindness you showed to others will unexpectedly come back to you"). Incarnation of psychological images was defined as "Whatever one believes in will materialize in real life," and there were five questions such as, "When you are anxious and think that 'Something bad will happen to me,' that thought will materialize. One's imagination has the power to make things happen in reality."

In the present analysis, we excluded middle and high school students and only analyzed the data from young adults (18-25 years old; n = 1,569 (48.5%)), middle-aged (26-64 years old; n = 1,038 (32.1%)), and older adults (65 and older; n = 627 (19.4%)). Their religious affiliation was as follows[3]: "Not religious" = 1,373 (45.3%), "Buddhist" = 642 (21.2%), "Christian" = 1,014 (33.5%).[4] However, we excluded those who claimed to have multiple religious affiliations (e.g., "I am both a Christian and a Buddhist") from the subsequent analyses and ended up with a total of 3,029 participants.[5]

To examine the relationship among age, religious affiliation, and spirituality, we conducted a statistical analysis (two-factor multivariate analysis of variance and simple main effect analyses) with three age groups (young adult, middle-aged, and old) and three religious affiliation groups (Buddhist, Christian, and non-religious) as independent variables and three subscales of the JSI (Meaning of life, Incarnation of psychological images, and Karma,) as dependent variables (see Table 9.3).

The analyses revealed several significant main and interaction effects for all the JSI subscales, and a few interesting trends emerged. First, when looking at the age group, it was found that the younger generations tend to undervalue all the spirituality factors.[6] One possible reason is the

Table 9.3 Means (Standard Deviations), Frequency Distribution, and F Values for Subscales of the Japanese Spirituality Index

		Young adult			Middle adult			Older adult			Main effect		Interaction
		Buddhist	Christian	Not religious	Buddhist	Christian	Not religious	Buddhist	Christian	Not religious	F (df)		F (df)
Meaning of life	Mean	19.56	20.53	18.75	22.50	20.54	19.51	21.69	21.68	19.18	23.51 ** (2, 2,968)	37.82 ** (2, 2,968)	13.46 ** (4, 2,968)
	SD	3.73	3.66	3.57	3.12	3.39	3.80	2.97	2.92	2.94			
	n	228	91	1143	246	515	168	157	390	39			
Karma	Mean	15.56	14.69	14.53	17.42	13.97	15.08	16.99	15.76	15.23	10.80 ** (2, 2,985)	56.71 ** (2, 2,985)	12.43 ** (4, 2,985)
	SD	3.21	3.56	3.33	2.57	3.55	3.26	2.36	3.02	2.75			
	n	231	93	1156	246	515	168	158	388	39			
Incarnation of psychological images	Mean	17.62	16.94	16.98	20.53	16.53	18.02	19.97	18.62	18.05	22.38 ** (2, 2,970)	43.64 ** (2, 2,970)	13.47 ** (4, 2,970)
	SD	4.02	4.77	3.91	3.46	4.28	3.92	2.84	3.69	2.80			
	n	227	93	1150	244	514	167	157	388	39			

Test of simple main effect

		Age groups	Religious groups
Meaning of life	Buddhist	Older adult, Middle adult > Young adult **	Young adult: Buddhist, Christian > Not religious **
	Christian	Older adult > Middle adult, Young adult **	Middle adult: Buddhist > Christian > Not religious **
	Not religious	Middle adult > Young adult *	Older adult: Buddhist, Christian > Not religious **
Karma	Buddhist	Older adult, Middle adult > Young adult **	Young adult: Buddhist > Not religious **
	Christian	Older adult > Middle adult **, Young adult *	Middle adult: Buddhist > Not religious > Christian **
	Not religious		Older adult: Buddhist > Christian, Not religious **
Incarnation of psychological images	Buddhist	Older adult, Middle adult > Young adult **	Young adult: Buddhist > Not religious > Christian **
	Christian	Older adult > Middle adult, Young adult **	Middle adult: Buddhist > Not religious > Christian **
	Not religious	Middle adult > Young adult **	Older adult: Buddhist > Christian**, Not religious*

** $p < .01$ * $p < .05$

interaction of a unique Japanese culture and the identity development suggested by F. Oser and J. W. Fowler among others. In contemporary Japan with regard to religion, people are more activity-oriented than ideology-oriented (e.g., visiting both Buddhist temple and *Shinto* shrine on the New Year's Day without believing in either religion). However, the spiritual concepts described here have strong ideological connotations (especially that of Buddhism), and the younger people may not have had enough opportunities to explore and make a commitment to a certain religious identity. For example, if one grows up in a typical Japanese household which is not very religious, he or she will have plenty of opportunities by the age of 30s and 40s to engage in many "religious" activities or to experience such life events as family tragedies which often facilitate the awareness of the meanings of these behaviors and their implications. In fact, our data revealed that the middle-aged and older adults both in Buddhist and Christian groups valued these spiritual dimensions more than the younger group. Even among those who are non-religious, the same pattern was found (except *Karma*), indicating an intertwined relationship between spirituality and identity development.

Second, there are also few notable findings when comparing the religious groups.[7] For the Buddhist group, every cohort scored significantly higher than the non-religious counterpart on the entire spirituality index except for the younger Buddhist group, which failed to score higher than the non-religious on Incarnation of psychological images. This is the aspect of spirituality that refers to a positive attitude and a belief in one's effort ("Whatever one believes in will materializes in real life"). These are the generations that had grown up in the dismal social and economic climate after the Japanese bubble economy burst in the 1980s, and perhaps that made them lose faith in not only the system but also in themselves. They are the so-called "lost generation" who gave up on "trying" in the society that failed them repeatedly. This result is consistent with another study in which Takahashi (2014) found that the younger people in Japan are pessimistic about their lives and prefer a medium that is pre-packaged and unrealistic but claims to provide "healing" to arduous spiritual struggles. They are the ones who seek healings (*iyashi*) from such media as "spi-con" (spiritual convention) and "spi-ma" (spiritual market where occult related goods are sold/exchanged).

Further, the Christian group scored significantly higher than the non-religious group only on Meaning of life. This makes sense if the participants thought of Christ as the one who gives "meaning and necessity (in life)" and understood this aspect of spirituality as similar to the Christian notion of providence or divine guidance. In contrast, compared to the Buddhist group, the Christian and non-religious groups scored significantly lower on Incarnation of psychological images and Karma, two concepts closely associated with the Buddhist teaching. For the Christians and non-religious individuals, these Buddhist values must be a world apart from what they believe.

7. Conclusion

In this chapter, I first reviewed the history, meanings, and cross-cultural data of spirituality. I then clarified the uniqueness and importance of spirituality as a psychological construct and discussed its values and potentials in the field of empirical science. It became clear through the discussion that the phonetically translated Japanese spirituality is a challenging concept to social scientists. While the scientific and folk definitions of many psychological concepts are not always identical, the discrepancy between the two regarding the concept of spirituality is too substantial to ignore. For example, many spiritual care professionals (e.g., religious and clinical professionals) recently reported that they were asked to perform occult rituals (communicating with deceased, clairvoyance, fortune telling, etc.) by people who regard spirituality as some sort of paranormal power. As we move on, it is imperative that we do not disregard but instead incorporate this unique notion of Japanese spirituality into the original "spirituality" (i.e., notion based on *spiritus*, *seishin-sei*, and *rei-sei*). While we must continue disseminating research findings to the general public, it is also important to further examine how Japanese people understand this concept. For this reason, our nation-wide research effort as a part of the J-MARS project was a valuable first step as it not only examined spirituality from the current scientific research but also extracted its meanings from a comprehensive list of popular Japanese books.

Finally, I also suggested throughout this chapter to continue the conceptual exploration of the relationship between spirituality and religiosity for the advancement of empirical research in this field. For example, I suggest that we emphasize "spirituality" by calling this field "Psychology of Religion and Spirituality" (instead of "Psychology of Religion" as usually designated in Japan). While the scientific community in Japan is understandably reluctant to include "spirituality" in the names of their organizations and journals since the Japanese spirituality carries extremely unscientific and cultish nuances due to its usage in popular culture, I believe it is more important to purposely foreground the word "spirituality," to increase Japanese recognition of the term and to accurately reflect what this field is about, as Division 36 of the American Psychological Association did in 2012. Such a bold move would facilitate a paradigm shift in Japan and could expand further interest in studying spirituality.

Notes:

[1] These names were generated during the study in 2000.

[2] Significant here means that according to the statistical analysis the average points for Hitler and Saddam Hussein were higher for the Japanese than the American group, and this difference is unlikely to be by chance (less than 5%).

[3] The actual question is as follows: *Do you have faith in a specific religion?*
Please circle the most appropriate number.
If you belong to a specific denomination, please indicate it in (   ):
1. Buddhism (Denomination:)
2. *Shinto* (Denomination:)
3. Christian (Denomination:)
4. Others (Denomination:)
5. I don't have faith.

[4] The total sample size was 3,234 (young: 1,569, middle-aged: 1038, older: 627), but there were 205 invalid responses.

[5] Although the research "field" of the J-MARS project includes *Izumo-Taisha-kyo* (Shinto), *Soto* sect and Rishokosei-kai (Buddhism), Catholic and Holiness (Protestant) church (Christian), we categorized the participants not based on these "fields" but their responses to the question of their religious organization.

[6] The results of simple main effect of age group, after performing two factor MANOVA were as follows. Meaning of life: Buddhist $F(2, 2968) = 45.66, p < .01$, Christian $F(2, 2968) = 13.34, p < .01$, non-religious $F(2, 2968) = 3.78, p < .05$, Karma: Buddhist $F(2, 2985) = 21.19, p < .01$, Christian $F(2, 2968) = 34.08, p < .01$, and Incarnation of psychological images: Buddhist $F(2, 2970) = 35.65, p < .01$, Christian $F(2, 2970) = 32.72, p < .01$, non-religious $F(2, 2970) = 6.33, p < .01$. It should be noted that "$p < .01$" or "$p < .05$" denotes that "significant difference was found at 1% (or 5%)." In the two-factor MANOVA and other statistical analyses here and elsewhere, this means that the group differences in scores are unlikely to be by chance (i.e., less than 1% (5%) of chance occurrence).

[7] The results of simple main effect of religion, after performing two factor MANOVA were as follows. Meaning of life: Young $F(2, 2968) = 15.26$, $p < .01$, Middle-age $F(2, 2968) = 43.79$, $p < .01$, Older $F(2, 2968) = 9.82$, $p < .05$, Karma: Young $F(2, 2985) = 9.91$, $p < .01$, Middle-age $F(2, 2985) = 95.61$, $p < .01$, Older $F(2, 2985) = 9.68$, $p < .01$, and Incarnation of psychological images: Middle-age $F(2, 2970) = 87.76$, $p < .01$, Older $F(2, 2970) = 7.88$, $p < .01$.

Appendix

Overview of the Questionnaires Used in the J-MARS

Kobo Matsushima, The University of Tokyo

Chapters 3 through 9 are based on the results and analyses of the data obtained through the questionnaires in the J-MARS project. Thus, these results owe a great deal to how we identified/recruited the research participants and how we actually carried out the project. In this section, I present a brief overview of the participants and the procedure for administering the questionnaires. The readers are welcome to refer to Matsushima (2015) for a detailed overview of the J-MARS project itself. [1]

1. The Research Purpose

The primary purpose of the J-MARS was to investigate the relationship between religiosity/spirituality and mental health (subjective well-being) among non-religious and religious Japanese people from five organizations[2]: *Izumo-Taisha-Kyo* (*Shinto*), the *Soto* Sect (Buddhism), *Risho-Kosei-Kai* (Buddhism), the Catholic Church (Christianity) and the Holiness Protestant church (Christianity). The religious Japanese were further categorized into religious leaders and other believers in each organization.

2. Research Participants

There was a total of 8,977 questionnaires distributed, and 7,879 were returned. Among those returned, 6,769 agreed but 259 did not consent to participate in the study. In addition, 849 failed to fill out the consent forms while 2 provided invalid responses (they circled both "Agree" and "Disagree"). Among those who agreed to respond, 6,620 responses were valid while 151 were deemed invalid. Thus, this project used those 6,620 questionnaire results as its data. Among those who provided the valid responses, 2,390 were men, 4,184 women, and 46 were unknown. The overall average age was 27.4 years old ($SD=19.6$ and age range was between 12 and 93). The total number, gender, and the average age of the participants at each field site is described in Appendix Table 1. Note that we did not use random sampling. Instead, we relied on each project member's accessibility to the sample group. As a result, there could be systematic biases regarding the participants' demographic characteristics, and this may have influenced our analyses and discussion.

Appendix Table 1 The Number and Age of the Participants at Each Field Site

No.	Groups	Total	Men (%)	Women (%)	Unknown (%)	Mean	SD	Min	Max
1	General adults/ university students	316	88 (27.8)	224 (70.9)	4 (1.3)	31.4	13.8	18	77
2	Chatholic-affiliated university students	896	313 (34.9)	577 (64.4)	6 (0.7)	19.3	1.4	18	51
3	Protestant-affiliated university students	377	217 (57.6)	158 (41.9)	2 (0.5)	20.2	2.1	18	48
4	Buddhism-affiliated university students	119	87 (73.1)	32 (26.9)	-	19.7	1.8	18	30
5	*Izumo-taisha* Shintoists	42	12 (28.6)	30 (71.4)	-	52.7	15.5	23	75
6	*Izumo-taisha* Shintoist leaders	12	8 (66.7)	4 (33.3)	-	54.5	14.4	29	76
7	*Rissho-kosei-kai* Buddhists	251	13 (5.2)	232 (92.4)	6 (2.4)	62.8	9.3	30	84
8	*Rissho-kosei-kai* Buddhist leaders	58	40 (69.0)	18 (31.0)	-	57.4	5.7	43	68
9	*Soto* Buddhists	165	98 (59.4)	65 (39.4)	2 (1.2)	60.9	14.6	22	90
10	*Soto* Buddhist leaders	50	47 (94.0)	3 (6.0)	-	39.7	10.8	25	73
11	Catholics	70	28 (40.0)	42 (60.0)	-	61.0	15.1	27	85
12	Catholic leaders	66	27 (40.9)	38 (57.6)	1 (1.5)	67.0	15.9	32	88
13	Holiness Protestants	763	251 (32.9)	497 (65.1)	15 (2.0)	56.8	16.9	18	93
14	Holiness Protestants leaders	107	58 (54.2)	48 (44.9)	1 (0.9)	58.2	11.9	35	82
15	Public middle school students	89	47 (52.8)	39 (43.8)	3 (3.4)	14.9	0.3	14	15
16	Public high school students	397	211 (53.2)	180 (45.3)	6 (1.5)	16.8	1.0	15	18
17	All-boys Catholic middle/high school	845	845 (100.0)	-	-	15.4	1.5	12	18
18	All-girls Catholic middle/high school	961	-	961 (100.0)	-	14.9	1.5	12	18
19	All-girls Protestant middle/high school A	573	-	573 (100.0)	-	14.5	1.4	12	17
20	All-girls Protestant middle/high school B	463	-	463 (100.0)	-	15.9	0.9	14	18
	Total (All participants)	6,620	2,390 (36.1)	4,184 (63.2)	46 (0.7)	27.4	19.6	12	93

3. Research Procedure

1) Research period

November 2013 ~ March 2014

2) Research methods

We used three methods to administer the questionnaires:

A) Sending questionnaires directly to the participants via conventional mail.

B) Administering them at each site.

C) Asking personnel who were in charge at each site to administer them.

3) Ethical considerations

    This project was approved by the Committee on Ethics for Experimental Research on Human Subjects, Graduate School of Arts and Sciences/College of Arts and Sciences at the University of Tokyo.

4) The questionnaires

    There are two versions of the questionnaire, one used only for the Christian fields, except in Catholic and Protestant colleges, and the other for the rest of the field. They include the following scales: Religious View Scale (Kaneko, 1997), Religious Image Scale (Kobayashi & Sakai, 2015), Subjective Well-being Scale (Ito, Sagara, Ikeda, & Kawaura, 2003), Christianity Religious Consciousness Index (used only for the Christian fields, except in the Catholic and Protestant colleges) (Matsushima, 2011), Japanese Spirituality Index (JSI) (Gushiken et al., 2013), Religious Perspective on Nature Index (RPN) (open-ended), Mental Health Questionnaire (open-ended), and demographic questions.

4. A Few More Comments on the Research Participants

    There are a couple of points to consider about our research participants.

1) "Japanese" participants

    The research participants were all "Japanese" in principle; that is, we believe that they are all Japanese nationals residing in Japan. However, as noted above, some data were collected by someone other than the project members. As a result, there may have been a small number of non-Japanese who were fluent in Japanese in our sample.

2) Definition of the "believers"

    The "believers" are those participants who were associated with one of the five religious organizations in this study. Even though we designated them as "believers," they may not necessarily "believe" in a particular religion. For example, there could be catechumens in our sample who were exploring Christianity, and they might not necessarily have been "believers" in Christianity yet. Similarly, in the *Soto* Sect, there could be cases in which the parents, who are sect members (*danka*), asked their children, who may not identify themselves as Buddhists, to participate in the study. On the other hand, there could be "believers" who ended up in our "general adults/students" sample, simply because they were recruited from public schools and community centers.

Thus, the "believers" in the current context should be defined as, "those who are a part of or associated with a particular religious organization." It is important to note that one's actual belief was not a part of the operational definition of the "believers." For "religious leaders," although the degree of commitment each organization/sect requires from these leaders may vary, they do take leadership positions in that organization, and thus this designation is appropriate.

In summary, I wish to note that the way each chapter (from Chapter 3 to Chapter 9) treats the concept of "believer" may not be the same. There are some chapters that use the categorization in Appendix Table 1, while other chapters may add another piece of data considering whether or not responders are religious. The reader is encouraged to ascertain the different definitions used in each chapter.

Notes:

[1] The research report (Matsushima, 2015) can be downloaded (in PDF format) from the Society for Study of Psychology of Religion website (https://psychology-of-religion-japan.org/project/2012kaken_report.html)

[2] The research fields can be understood as those organizations with "strong" or "weak" religious overtones. We named the people associated with the former "believers," while those associated with the latter "general adults/students." However, as noted in (4) above (A Few Comments on the Research Participants), this distinction is extremely difficult to make, especially because how much of commitment is required to be a "believer" differs for each organization/sect.

References

Aizawa, S. (2016). Kaso-chiiki ni okeru kuyo to bodai-ji: Soto-shu [Current status of *Soto* Zen temples in depopulated areas]. In Sakurai, Y., & Kawamata, T. (Eds), *Jinko-gensho-shakai to jiin: Social-capital no siza kara*. Kyoto: Hozo-kan.

Allport, G.W. (1950). *The Individual and His Religion*. New York: Macmillan.

Ama, T. (1996). *Nihonjin wa naze mushukyo nanoka?* [Why Japanese are non-religious?]. Tokyo: Chikuma.

Ando, T. (2006). Ekkyo suru supirichuarithi [Transcending spirituality]. *Religious Studies in Japan, 349*, 73-92.

Arakawa, A. & Matsushima, K. (2016). Nihon ni okeru koudou eno shuukyo no eikyou to shuukyouhenoteikou [The impact of religion on behavior and resistance to having faith in Japan]. *Japanese Journal of Research on Emotions, 24*(supplement), os11.

Asoya, M. (1994). *Shinto towa nanika* [What is *Shintoism*?]. Tokyo: Perikan-sha.

Atran, S. & Norenzayan, A. (2004). Religion's evolutionary landscape: Counterintuition, commitment, compassion, communion. *Behavioral and Brain Sciences, 27*(6), 713-770.

Bruner, J. S. (1990). *Acts of meaning*. Cambridge: Harvard University Press.

Doi, T. (1973). *The anatomy of dependence*. (Trans. John Bester). Oxford, England: Kodansha international.

Elkins, D. N., Hedstrom, L. J., Hughes, L. L., Leaf, J. A., & Saunders, C. (1988). Toward a humanistic-phenomenological spirituality: Definition, description, and measurement. *Journal of Humanistic Psychology, 28*(4), 5-18.

Feder, A., Ahmad, S., Lee, E. J., Morgan, J. E., Singh, R., Smith, B. W., et al. (2013). Coping and PTSD symptoms in Pakistani earthquake survivors: Purpose in life, religious coping and social support. *Journal of Affective Disorders, 147*(1-3), 156-163.

Frank, A. (1995). *The wounded storyteller: Body, illness, and ethics*. Chicago: The University of Chicago Press.

Fujimaru, T. (2013). *Volunteer Souryo: Higashinihon daishinsai hisaichi no koewo kiku* [Volunteer monk]. Tokyo: Doubunkan.

Glock, C.Y. (1962). On the Study of Religious Commitment. *Religious Education Research* (Supplement), *57*, 98-110.

Gushiken, N. (2009). Sobokuna shinkonikansuru kisokenkyu IV [Research on folk spirituality]. *Japan Psychological Association Conference Abstract*, 1104-1105.

Gushiken, N., Matsushima, K., Hirako, Y., Tokuno, Y., Aizawa, S., & Sakai, K. (2013). Shuukyo-sei/supirichuariti to seishinteki kenkou no kanren [Relationship between religiosity/spirituality and mental health]. *Japanese Social Psychology Conference Abstract*, 210.

Haebara, T. (2001). Ryoutekichousa: shakudo no sakusei to soukanbunseki [Quantitative survey: Scale composition and correlation analysis]. In T. Haebara, S. Ichikawa, & H. Shimoyama (Eds.), *Shrinrigaku kenkyuho nyumon* (pp. 63-91). Tokyo: University of Tokyo Press.

Haebara, T., Ichikawa, S., & Shimoyama, H. (Eds.). (2001). *Shrinrigaku kenkyuho nyumon: chosa, jikken kara jissen made* [Introduction to Research Method in Psychology: Surveys, Experiments and Practices]. Tokyo: University of Tokyo Press.

Hardy, A. (1979). *The spiritual nature of man*. Oxford: Religious Experience Research Centre.

Haya, T. (2011). *Gautama Buddha no message* [Message from Gautama Buddha]. Tokyo: Taizo shuppan.

Hayashi, C. (1996). *Nihon rashisa no kozo: Kokoro to bunka wo hakaru* [The structure of Japaneseness]. Tokyo: Toyo keizaishinpo.

Hayashi, F. (2010). Gendai nihonjin ni totteno shinko no umu to shuukyouteki na kokoro [Contemporary Japanese Religious Mind]. *Proceedings of the Institute of Statistical Mathematics, 58* (1), 39-59.

Hayashi, F. (2012). Sobokuna shukyo-teki kanjo ni kansuru chosa de kangaeta koto [Thoughts based on a research about folk religious emotions]. *Shin Joho, 100*, 12-19.

Higuchi, K. (2014). *Shakai chosa no tameno keiryo tekisuto bunseki* [Text analysis for social studies]. Kyoto: Nakanishiya.

Hood, R. W., Hill, P. C. & Williamson, W. P. (2005). *The psychology of religious fundamentalism*. New York: Guilford Press.

Hori, S. (1991). Shogai Hattatsuron to Kyouiku [Theory of lifespan development and education]. *Bulletin of the Nagoya University College of the Faculty of Education: The Department of Educational Psychology, 38*, 16-19.

Hoshino, A. (1977). Shukyo ishiki no hattatsu [Development of religious consciousness]. In A. Yoda. (Ed.). *Shin Kyoiku sinrigaku jiten* (pp. 376-377). Tokyo: Kaneko Shobo

Ienaga, S. (1997). *Nihon shisoushi ni okeru shukyo teki shizenkan no tenkai* (Vol. 1) [Religious views on nature in the history of Japanese ideologies]. Tokyo: Iwanami.

Ikeuchi, H. & Fujiwara, T. (2009). Soshitu karano shinriteki kaifuku katei [Psychological recovery process from a loss]. *Japanese Journal of Social Psychology 24*(3), 169-178.

International Institute for the Study of Religions (IISR) (Ed.). (1996). *Hanshin awaji daishinsai to shukyo* [The *Hanshin-Awaji* earthquake and religion]. Osaka: Toho.

International Institute for the Study of Religions (IISR) (Ed.). (2013). *Gendai syukyo 2013:3.11 go wo hiraku* [Contemporary religion 2013]. Tokyo: Akiyama-shoten.

Ishii, K. (2007). *Databook gendai-nihon-jin no shukyo zoho-kaitei-ban* [Contemporary-Japanese religion]. Tokyo: Shinyo-sha.

Isomae, J. (2003). *Kindai-nihon no shukyo-gensetsu to sono keihu: Shukyo, kokka, shinto* [Religious discourse and its genealogy in modern Japan: Religion, state, and *shinto*]. Tokyo: Iwanami.

ISSP Research Group (2018). International Social Survey Programme: Religion III-ISSP 2008. *GESIS Data Archive, Cologne. ZA4950 Data file Version 2.3.0*.

Ito, Y., Sagara, J., Ikeda, M., & Kawaura, Y. (2003). Shukanteki koufukukan shakudo no sakusei to shinraisei to datousei no kentou [Reliability and validity of a subjective well-being scale]. *Japanese Journal of Psychology, 74*(3), 276-281.

James, W. (1902). *The variety of religious experience*. New York: New American Library.

Kan, S-J. (2015, June 20). Shuukyou wo yomitoku chikara [Ability to understand religion]. *The Asahi Shimbun*, p.10.

Kaneko, S. (1997). *Nihon-jin no shukyo-sei: Okage to tatari no shakai-sinri-gaku* [The Japanese religious characters]. Tokyo: Shinyo-sha.

Kawashima, D. (2011). Shukyo shinrigaku ni okeru shitsutekikenkyu no hohoron to sono kanousei [Qualitative methodology and the possibilities in religious psychology]. In S. Kaneko, Y. Kono, R. Nishiwaki, S. Sugiyama & K. Matsushima (Eds.), *Shukyo shinrigaku gairon* (pp. 23-24). Kyoto: Nakanishiya.

King, P. E., & Boyatzis, C. J. (2015). Religious and spiritual development. In M. E. Lamb (Ed.), Socioemotional Processes (pp. 975-1021). *Handbook of child psychology and developmental science (Vol. 3)*. Hoboken, New Jersey: Willey.

Kishimoto, H. (1961). *Shuukyougaku* [Religious Studies]. Tokyo: Taimeido.

Kitamura, T. (2013). *Kuen: Higashinihon daishinsai yorisou shukyosha tachi* [Excruciating fate]. Tokyo: Tokuma-shoten.

Kobayashi, M., & Sakai, K. (2015). *Shuukyo/supirichuarithi no jittaihaaku* [Meaning of religion and spirituality]. In K. Matsushima (Ed.). Project report (the relationship between religiosity/spirituality and mental health: An empirical study of Hardships and resilience), the Japanese Grant-in-aid for Scientific Research (#24330185), 31-36.

Koenig, H. (2008). *Medicine, religion, and health: Where science and spirituality meet*. West Conshohocken, PA: Templeton Foundation Press.

Komatsu, K. (2002). *Kaminaki-jidai no minzokugaku* [Ethnology in the era of no God]. Tokyo: Serika-shobo.

Koyasu, M. (2011). Hattatsu shinrigaku towa [What is developmental psychology?]. In T. Muto & M. Koyasu (Eds.). *Hattatsu shinrigaku I* (pp. 1-37). Tokyo: University of Tokyo Press.

Manabe, K. (2010). Shuko-ishiki no kouzo: Nihon to Doitsu niokeru kokusai hikaku [The Structure of Religiosity: An International Comparison of Japan and Germany]. *Journal of Japan Association for Public Opinion Research, 105*, 3-10.

Markus, H. R., & Kitayama, S. (1991). Culture and the self: Implications for cognition, emotion, and motivation. *Psychological review, 98*(2), 224-253.

Maruya, S. (1999). *Atarashii katachi no jiritsu no jissen* [New practice to become independent]. Tokyo: Life Planning Center Foundation.

Maslow, A. H. (1943). A theory of human motivation. *Psychological Review, 50,* 370-396.

Matsumoto, S. (1979). *Shuukyou shinrigaku* [Psychology of Religion]. University of Tokyo Press.

Matsushima, K. (2011). *Shuukyousei no hattatsu shinrigaku* [Developmental Psychology of Religiosity]. Kyoto: Nakanishiya.

Matsushima, K. (2012). Nihon ni okeru jisshouteki shukyo shinrigakuteki [Empirical psychology of religion in Japan: past, present and future]. *The World of Psychology, 59,* 9-12.

Matsushima, K. (2014). Shukyousei [Religiosity]. In M. Goto, K. Ninomiya, H. Takagi, H.Ono, T. Shirai, K. Hiraishi, Y. Satoh & Y. Wakamatsu (Eds.). *Shin seinen sinrigaku handobukku* (pp. 234-246). Tokyo: Fukumura.

Matsushima, K. (Ed.) (2015). Project report (the relationship between religiosity/spirituality and mental health: An empirical study of hardships and resilience), the Japanese Grant-in-aid for Scientific Research (#24330185).

Matsushima, K. & Arakawa, A. (2015). *Shinko-no-hituyo-sei-ninchi/ shinko-no-umu-to-sekaikan oyobi shukanteki koufukukan tono kankei* [The relationship between perceived needs for faith / presence or absence of faith and understanding of the world/subjective well-being]. [Conference Session]. Convention of the Japanese Psychological Association 79th Annual Convention.

McNamee, S., & Gergen, K. J. (1992). *Therapy as social construction*. London: Sage Publication.

Meisenhelder, J. B. (2002). Terrorism, posttraumatic stress, and religious coping. *Issues in Mental Health Nursing, 23*(8), 771–782.

Miki, H. (Ed.). (2001). *Fukko to shukyo: Shinsaigo no hito to shakai wo iyasumono* [Reconstruction and religion]. Osaka: Toho-shuppan.

Mitsuhashi, T. (2007). *Shinto no joushiki ga wakaru shojiten* [Encyclopedia to understand common sense of *Shintoism*]. Tokyo: PHP Interface.
Miyatake, S. & Higuchi, M. (2017). Does religious priming increase the prosocial behaviour of a Japanese sample in an anonymous economic game? *Asian Journal of Social Psychology, 20*(1), 54-59.
Morioka, M. (2008). *Narrative to Shinri-Ryouhou* [Narrative and Psychotherapy]. Tokyo: Kongo-shuppan.
Murai, J. (Ed.), (2012). *Progress and application: Shinrigaku kenkyuho* [Progress & application: Psychological research methods]. Tokyo: Saiensu-sha.
Nakao, M. (2012). Ippantaishu ni okeru bukkyo shinko no ichi sokumen-Jiin sanpai to shakyo ni yoru shinriteki henyo [Faith of Buddhism in Japanese]. *Journal of Buddhist Culture, 21-22,* 43-57.
NHK Broadcasting Culture Research Institute (Ed.). (2015). *Gendai nihonjin no ishiki kozo* [The Structure of the Consciousness of Contemporary Japanese 8th edition]. Tokyo: NHK Publishing.
Nishida, K. (2008). *Shinjiru kokoro no kagaku* [Science of beliefs]. Tokyo: Saiensusya.
Nishimura, A. (2013). Junshoku-keikan no irei to kensho: Junsa-daimyojin Masuda Keitaro no baai [Memorization of fallen police offices: In the case of Masuda Keitaro]. In K. Murakami & A. Nishimura (Eds.), *Irei no keifu: Shisha wo kiokusuru kyodotai* (pp. 95-126). Tokyo: Shinwa-sha.
Nishiwaki, R. (2004). *Nihonjin no shukyo-teki shizenkan: Ishiki chusa ni yoru jisshou-teki kenkyu.* [The religious view of nature among Japanese: An empirical study based on an attitude survey]. Kyoto: Minerva.
Nishiwaki, R. (2005). Shukyosei hattatsu kenkyu no kenkyu doko [Research trends in the study of religiosity development]. In M. Urakami, S. Kamiya & K. Nakamura (Eds.), *Shinrigaku: Introduction to psychology* (pp. 122-123). Kyoto: Nakanishiya.
Nölke, M. (2014). *Nihonjin ni shukyo wa iranai* [Religions are unnecessary for Japanese]. Tokyo: Best Sellers.
NPO organization *Hanshin awaji daisinsai 1.17 kibou no akari, Mainichi shinbun shuzai han.* (2004). *Omoide kizande: Shinsai 10 nen no monument* [Engraving the memories]. Osaka: Dorimu.
Ohishi, S. (2006). Bunka to Well-being [Culture and well-being]. In S. Shimai (Ed.), *Positive shinrigaku-21seiki no shinrigaku no kanosei* (pp. 114-131). Kyoto: Nakanishiya.
Ohmura, T. (2010). Omukae-gensho to shinriryoho: Shi no bunka to Spiritual Care [Omukae phenomena and psychotherapy]. *Japan Society of Spiritual Care Newsletter, 3,* 20-24.
Ohnishi, K. (1948). *Shizen kanjo no ruikei* [Typology of feeling about nature]. Tokyo: Kaname-shobo.
Onda, A. (2010). Bukyo no inori to jihi no meiso [Forgiveness and meditation in Buddhism]. *Journal of Buddhism Psychology, 1,* 158-160.
Park, C. L. (2014). Religions and meaning. In R. F. Palouzian & C. L. Park (Eds.), *Handbook of psychology of religion and spirituality* (2nd. ed.) (pp. 357-379). New York: Guilford Press.
Preston, J. & Epley, N. (2009). Science and God: An automatic opposition between ultimate explanations. *Journal of Experimental Social Psychology, 45,* 238-241.
Rambo, L. R. (1993). *Understanding religious conversion.* New Haven, CT: Yale University Press.

Reuder, M. E. (1999). A history of division 36. In D. A. Dewsbury (Ed.), *Unification through division: Histories of the divisions of the American Psychological Association* (Vol. 4) (pp. 91-108). Washington, DC: American Psychological Association.

Ribaudo, A. & Takahashi, M. (2009). Temporal trends in spirituality research: A meta-analysis of journal abstract between 1944 and 2003, In Ellor, J. (Ed.), *Methods in religion, spirituality, and aging* (pp. 13-25). Oxon, Oxford: Routledge.

Saijo, T. (2002). The narrative of nature, weather, and season in face of death: A model of the life story research to succeed previous hypotheses. *Japanese Journal of Qualitative Psychology, 1,* 55-69.

Satake, A., Yamada, H., Kudo, R., Otani, M., & Yamasaki, F. (2013). *Manyoushu.* Tokyo: Iwanami.

Sato, T. (2009). TEM de hajimeru shitsuteki kenkyu [Qualitative research with TEM method]. In T. Sato (Ed.), *TEM de hajimeru shituteki kenkyu* (pp. 92-101). Tokyo: Seishin-shobo.

Sawada, A. (2015, June 20). Be between Dokusha to tsukuru: kami ya hotoke wo shinjimasuka. [Do you believe in god?]. *The Asahi Shimbun,* p.10.

Seki, K. (1944). *Nihon jido shukyo no kenkyu* [Research on religion among Japanese children]. Tokyo: Shoko-shoin.

Shariff, A. F., & Norenzayan, A. (2007). God is watching you: Priming god concepts increases prosocial behavior in an anonymous economic game. *Psychological Science, 18,* 803-809.

Shimada, H. (2009). *Mushukyo koso nihonjin no shukyo dearu* [Non-religion is the Japanese religion]. Tokyo: Kadokawa.

Shimazono, S. (2012). *Gendai shukyo to supirichuariti* [Contemporary religions and spirituality]. Tokyo: Kobun-do.

Shimai, S. (1997). *Kenko shinrigaku* [Health psychology]. Tokyo: Baihukan.

Shimai, S. (2009). *Positive shinrigaku* [Positive psychology]. Tokyo: Seiwa

Singelis, T. M., Triandis, H. C., Bhawuk, D. P., & Gelfand, M. J. (1995). Horizontal and vertical dimensions of individualism and collectivism: A theoretical and measurement refinement. *Cross-Cultural Research, 29*(3), 240-275.

Survey Committee of Current Status for *Soto* Zen Buddhism Temples. (Ed.). (2014). *Soto-shu danshinto-ishiki-chosa hokoku-sho* [The attitude survey on the "believers" in *Soto* Zen Buddhism]. Tokyo: *Soto-shu* shumu-cho.

Takahashi, K. (2012). Hattatsu towa [What is development?] In K. Takahashi, R. Yukawa, J. Ando & H. Akiyama (Eds.). *Hattatsukagaku nyumon I: Riron to hoho* [Developmental science I: Concepts, theories and methods] (pp. 3-19). Tokyo: University of Tokyo Press.

Takahashi, M. (2011a). Shukyo to supirichuariti [Religion and spirituality]. In S. Kaneko, K. Matsushima, Y. Kono, S. Sugiyama, & R. Nishiwaki (Eds.), *Shukyo sinrigaku gairon* (pp. 61-80). Kyoto: Nakanishiya.

Takahashi, M. (2011b*)*. Saikou—3 sedai hikaku ni yoru spupirichuariti no imi [Meanings of spirituality re-visited: A follow-up study among three generations in Japan]. *Japanese Journal of Gerontology, 33*(2), 221.

Takahashi, M. (2014). Koureika to shukyo no rounengakuteki oyobi shinrigakuteki kousatsu [Gerontological and psychological perspectives on aging and religion]. *Gendai Shuko.* Tokyo: International Religious Research Institute.

Takahashi, M. (2019). Relationship between wisdom and spirituality: An expanded theoretical model with mysticism and gerotranscendence. In J. Gluck and R. J. Sternberg (Eds.), *The handbook of wisdom* (pp. 626-646). New York: Cambridge University Press.

Takahashi, M., Acosta, P., Buttitta, G., Carr-Williams, C., Durczak, S., Gray-Abdai, S., & Sullivan, S. M. (2000, November). *Implicit theories of spirituality: Their religious boundary and characteristics.* [Poster presentation]. 53rd Annual Meeting of the Gerontological Society of America, Washington, DC.

Takahashi, M. & Ide. S. (2003). Implicit Theories Across Three Generations: A Cross-Cultural Comparison in the U.S. and Japan. *Journal of Religious Gerontology, 15*(4), 15-38.

Takahashi, M. & Ide. S. (2004). Supirichuarithi no imi. [Meaning of spirituality]. *Japanese Journal of Gerontology, 26*(3), 296-307.

Takano, Y. & Oka, T. (Eds.). (2004). *Shinrigaku kenkyuho - kokoro wo mitsumeru kagaku nomanazashi* [Research Methods in Psychology: Scientific Eyes on Mind]. Tokyo: Yuhikaku.

Takeda, Y. & Nakamura, H. (1999). *Kojiki.* Tokyo: Kadokawa Sophia Bunko.

Tomohisa, H. (2010). Bukkyo to counseling [Buddhism and counseling]. In H. Tomohisa (Ed.), *Bukkyo to counseling* (pp.5-15). Kyoto: Hozokan.

Tsuchihash, H. (1990). *Nihongo ni saguru kodai shinkou: Fetishism kara Shinto made* [Searching Ancient *Shintoism* in Japanese Language]. Tokyo: Chuo koron shinsha.

Tsuruoka, Y. (2004). *Ken'i, dento, sinko* [Authority, tradition, and belief]. Tokyo: Iwanami.

Wakimoto, R. (2012). *Sonzai kyoui kanri riron eno sasoi* [Introduction to Terror management theory]. Tokyo: Saiensu-sha.

Wuthnow, R. (2007). *America and the challenges of religious diversity.* Princeton, N.J.: Princeton University Press.

Yamada, Y. (2000). *Jinsei wo monogataru: Seisei no life story* [Narrating one's life]. Kyoto: Minerva.

Yamada, Y. (2003). Fieldwork to shitsuteki shinri kenkyuho no kisoenshu [Basic practice of the fieldwork and qualitative research in psychology]. *The Annual Bulletin of Praxis and Research Center for Clinical Psychology and Education 49,* 22-45.

Yamada, Y. (2007). *Soushitu no katari: Seisei no lifestory* [Narrative on loss: lifestory for generation]. Tokyo: Shinyo-sha.

Yanaihara, T. (2012). *Kirisutokyo nyumon* [Introduction of Christianity] (pp. 114-121). Tokyo: Chukou-kouron-shinsha.

Editor

Masami Takahashi is a professor of psychology and gerontology at Northeastern Illinois University. The author of numerous articles and book chapters both in English and Japanese, Dr. Takahashi studies psychological strengths in late adulthood (e.g., wisdom and spirituality) across cultures and their potential roles in longevity. He also produced and directed a documentary film, *The Last Kamikaze: Testimonials from the WWII Suicide Pilots*.